All Together Now!

All Together Now!

A Seriously Fun Collection of Training Games and Activities

LORRAINE L. UKENS

Jossey-Bass
Pfeiffer
San Francisco

ISBN: 0-7879-4503-X

Library of Congress Cataloging-in-Publication Data
Ukens, Lorraine L.
All together now!: a seriously fun collection of training
games and activities / Lorraine L. Ukens.
p. cm.
ISBN 0-7879-4503-X (acid-free paper)
1. Employees—Training of. 2. Experiential learning. 3.
Educational games. I. Title.
HF5549.5.T7 U4 1999
659.3′124—dc21   99-6036

Published by

350 Sansome Street, 5th Floor
San Francisco, California 94104-1342
(415) 433-1740; Fax (415) 433-0499
(800) 274-4434; Fax (800) 569-0443

Visit our website at: www.pfeiffer.com

Acquiring Editor: Matthew Holt
Director of Development: Kathleen Dolan Davies
Developmental Editor: Susan Rachmeler
Editor: Rebecca Taff
Senior Production Editor: Dawn Kilgore
Manufacturing Supervisor: Becky Carreño
Interior Design & Illustrations: Gene Crofts
Cover Design: Tom Morgan/Blue Design

Printing   10 9 8 7 6 5 4 3 2 1

 This book is printed on acid-free, recycled stock that meets or exceeds the minimum GPO and EPA requirements for recycled paper.

To Leon

For your belief and understanding

For your support and encouragement

For your ideas and inspiration

Contents

Introduction

Activities

Introduction

Introduction

Experiential Learning

We do; therefore we learn. Few can argue that experience is the richest resource for adult learning. People retain knowledge more easily when they experience things in an unforgettable way. Games and other hands-on exercises help induce this result in training situations. Experiential learning involves active participation in a planned series of events, an analysis of what is experienced, and the application of the experiences to work and life situations.

The idea behind experiential training is to put people in situations that do not look like work, but that actually contain analogies to situations they are likely to encounter on the job. It allows participants the opportunity to take a close look at themselves and how they do things. They can think back to what made them act or react in a certain way on the job or in personal relationships and walk away with a new mind-set as to how to respond to an actual situation when it comes up. The ability to transfer the learning back to the workplace is critical; training is only effective if the participant can *apply* the information. A training "experience" turns the event into an interactive form of learning, as the individual makes the actual cognitive link, not the trainer or "teacher." This method is very effective in helping participants learn, because the lesson becomes an integral part of the participants' lives.

The facilitator must remember that adult learners share certain characteristics. They have strong feelings about learning situations in general. Because they have a good deal of first-hand experience, they bring along a wealth of ideas to contribute. Adult learners also have established values, attitudes, and tendencies. This means that they have set habits and strong tastes that affect their learning. Most importantly, adults generally have more to lose. They have a high degree of pride and may fear a loss of respect as well as reputation. Experiential activities, when used properly and sensitively, can help alleviate many of the fears that adults associate with the learning process and allow for a comfortable environment of discovery. Participants can be given opportunities to explore new views and practice new skills in a safe, low-risk environment.

Experiential Learning Cycle[1]

Experiential learning can be viewed as a dynamic sequence of events. The cycle begins with *the event itself*, as experienced by the participant. This provides the basis for the discussion that comes afterward. Because all the participants have been provided with the same experience, they are able to focus on a common base.

The next four phases of the cycle constitute the debriefing or feedback session, which helps people make the connection between the activity and what is to be learned from it. Debriefing of the experience should begin by having individuals *share feelings, reactions, and observations* about the event itself. Next comes a discussion of *what happened in general*. The group as a whole examines the interactions, patterns, and group dynamics that may have occurred. This is a pivotal step in the debriefing process and is critical for the connection between the event and real-life situations.

Participants then begin to *generalize* about what has been learned from the experience. By identifying patterns, participants can abstract inferences, generalizations, learnings, and principles that apply to their own lives. This is the time to introduce the actual concepts being taught. The final stage involves *application* of what was learned, at which time participants plan more effective behavior for the future. This is where the transfer of skills from the classroom to the workplace occurs. Some of the more common methods utilized to achieve this objective include goal setting and action planning.

Advantages of Experiential Learning

There are many advantages to learning experientially, especially the following:

- Learner-Based: The learner experiences something and sets his or her own learning pace;
- Process and Product: "How" something happens is as important as "what" happens;
- Holistic Understanding: The big picture is emphasized, rather than fragments of understanding;
- Multiple Relevance: Other relevant points can come up beyond the original objective;
- Personal Nature: The feelings, values, and perceptions of the learner are important;
- Flexibility: Conditions can be changed according to the needs of a group;
- Experimentation: Skills can be practiced;
- Anonymity: A safe environment is provided for individuals to participate;
- Full Participation: All participants are involved in the activity;

---

[1]Adapted from *The 1997 Reference Guide to Handbooks and Annuals.* San Francisco: Jossey-Bass/Pfeiffer.

- Peer Learning: Participants model behaviors, which promotes a group learning dynamic;
- Self-Directed Evaluation: Participants are encouraged to take responsibility for their own learning;
- Memorable: Participants recall the experience easily, thus retaining what they learned; and
- FUN!: Participants enjoy the experience.

Games as Experiential Activities

A Brief History of Games

The word *game* is directly linked to nature and animal concerns. It evolved from the Indo-European *ghem*, which described not only game-like activity but also the behavior of animals. The literal meaning was "to leap joyfully, to spring." An old Norse derivation, *gems*, meant "to come together and congregate as a school of whales do."

The word *gambol* still refers to the carefree frisking of a four-legged animal, and "game" is still what we hunt. Why this connection between animal antics and what we call games? Etymologists suggest that the antic behavior of herds of animals (and schools of whales) must have appeared to be carefree and pointless—and FUN. That's the feeling that is mirrored in the world of games.

The first organized games were undoubtedly riddles. The oldest recorded ones are Babylonian school texts. Riddles were used in important ceremonies in the ancient world. They were endowed with mystic importance, and it was thought that solving riddles would aid one in dealing with the greater problems of life and death.

Board games have been found in almost every culture, and over 270 different board games from ancient times have been documented. The first games were not considered idle play. They often had a higher religious purpose, mixing pleasurable pastimes with solemn respect for the vagaries of divine fate. The earliest known game board dates from 4000 to 3500 B.C. and was found in a predynastic cemetery in El-Mahasna, along with a pile of clay and ivory game pieces.

Games for Training and Development

Games are children's first attempts at group play. Youngsters demonstrate a liberated attitude that makes learning natural and spontaneous, probably because the process is uninhibited. In order for adults to learn in the same way, barriers inherent to the organizational culture need to be removed so that participants in training events share and enjoy learning in a natural manner. Games also serve as mechanisms for releasing learning and innovation that may lie dormant in many organizations. This is true for various reasons: Games raise people's awareness and make them more open to learning; they foster interactive and collaborative learning; and they persuade people to drop their guard and become engaged in learning. In addition, games are fun—an element that is too often missing from the workplace.

Games and simulations are experiential activities that have gained increasing acceptance in all levels of training and education and in a wide variety of subject areas.

However, some facilitators are still reluctant to use games during training events, because they feel that the participants will view the activities as merely fun and not relevant to learning. However, if the activity is treated sincerely and professionally, the participants actually will find that "games" encourage openness and present a unique way of looking at attitudes and behavior in a safe environment.

The fundamental defining feature of games and simulations is in the nature of the interactions (1) between participants and the situation, crisis, problem, or task and (2) among participants in the activity. The primary differences between educational games and those used for entertainment include: The application of curriculum-based knowledge and skills, the elimination of chance as the sole basis for winning, and the application of competition in teams rather than as individuals.

An ingrained belief in our society is that adult learners are supposed to be "in control"; therefore, they often display restricted emotional responses. Games can help break through participants' resistance. Games help take the participants' minds off outside pressures and lessen their anxiety about learning new things or facing controversial issues. A fun approach can even diminish some of the distractions that many workers feel when they must leave the work behind and go to a training event. They relax and listen better because the game format relieves some of their stress and breaks down their defensiveness. Joining in playful activities also provides people with a shared history and better sense of how to relate to one another.

Fundamentals

Organization of the Book

The games in this book are arranged alphabetically, for ease of use. Each activity includes the objective and appropriate topic areas, the recommended group size, approximate time required, a list of materials required, and preparation notes. To assist the facilitator in effectively conducting and debriefing the activity, step-by-step process notes are included, as well as discussion questions that associate the outcomes of the activity to particular concepts in the workplace. Where appropriate, templates of any necessary forms or materials are furnished. Some also contain information on how to vary the activity to create a different approach. Because each can apply to a variety of content areas, an Activity Topics Table has been provided at the end of this introduction as an easy-to-use guide for selecting an appropriate activity.

Choosing the Activity

Games must be used thoughtfully. They are not meant to be used only as a means of having fun, but as a means to an end. Facilitators must remember that they are using tools for instruction and must keep focusing on the results they want to achieve. Activities can succeed with any subject matter, any segment of the workforce, and any length training session. An activity may be used as the main learning event, or several may be used throughout the training session to reinforce or introduce any number of topics. Because they are so flexible, they offer the additional opportunity to vary conditions in accordance with the needs of a specific group. However, the activity must fit within the context of the whole instructional process.

This book provides learning games that can be used to reinforce fundamental concepts in fifteen basic areas: change, communication, conflict management, creativity, decision making, diversity, goal setting, icebreakers, leadership, negotiation, perception, planning, problem solving, resource use, and team dynamics. Each category is defined in Exhibit I.1 on page 8; Exhibit I.2 on page 10 shows the activities that are recommended for each specific topic.

For any given learning objective, there are many possible activities, differing in complexity and in the demands made of the participants. The facilitator should select activities that are most suitable for the intended audience. A wide variety of endeavors involve such things as solving problems and puzzles, making self-disclosure statements, role playing, creating art objects, and so forth. In addition, the activities may incorporate work as individuals, in pairs, triads, small groups, or large groups. The actual number of participants often limits the kind of activity that can be used. Environmental factors may also restrict playing conditions.

Group Size and Time Required

In general, the activities are very flexible in regard to group size and timing. The listed time required is only an approximation, as the length of the activity depends on several variables: the number of participants, the extent and style of the debriefing, and so on. A good guide to follow is that the larger the number of participants, the longer the activity will take. This is not a hard-and-fast rule, but it is a rather good indicator of what happens in larger groups, because the debriefing and reporting generally take longer.

Facilitator's Role

With experiential learning, the facilitator's main emphasis is to assist in a process of inquiry, analysis, and decision making with learners, rather than merely to transmit knowledge. He or she must be able to help the participants make the connection between the experience and the intent of the learning. Therefore, it is important that the activity itself be set up, run, and processed properly with a and tie back to the real world. For the games to have educational value, there must be a good match between the metaphors or analogies of the event and real-life issues. The joy of full discovery generally comes after the game or even after the participant leaves the session.

Unless the activity calls for the facilitator to take an active role, the participants should be allowed to experience the event on their own. They should be allowed the freedom to make mistakes, because this in itself is an excellent way to analyze the situation and learn from the experience. Facilitators should intervene only on questions of procedure and only to give as much information as possible to clarify a situation without influencing the outcome.

Debriefing

The facilitator must emphasize the instructional message, in addition to the fun, so that participants take the training seriously. The debriefing is the critical point at which to make connections with the real world of work. The debriefing must be interactive. The

Exhibit I.1. Definitions of Fundamental Concepts

Change: Ability to be flexible, adaptable, and open to new ideas in order to understand and react to changing environments and situations.

Communication: Transmission of information and understanding between individuals, including how people talk, listen, and put forth their ideas.

Conflict Management: Process of managing differences among ideas, perceptions, beliefs, and goals of individuals.

Creativity: Ability to be inventive, imaginative, or original.

Decision Making: Process of identifying and evaluating potential courses of action, then choosing from the various options.

Diversity: Quality of having difference or variety.

Goal Setting: Establishment of a direction for action or a specific quantity of work to be accomplished.

Icebreaker: Means for individuals to mix together or become better acquainted with one another.

Leadership: Ability to influence and direct the behaviors of others.

Negotiation: Reciprocal bargaining process that is a basis of agreement between opposing parties.

Perception: View individuals have of things in the world around them and its effect on concept formation and behavior.

Planning: Use of strategies, objectives, and specifications that precede an action.

Problem Solving: Use of skills to solve something capable of solution, such as a puzzle, as well as coping with difficulties that present problems in real life.

Resource Use: Interpretation of data and information, as well as use of available supplies.

Team Dynamics: Impact of group structure on member actions, social interaction, and cohesiveness.

facilitator must lead people to insights by discussing, reflecting, and questioning what was experienced. Rather than *telling* the participants the learning points, an effective facilitator guides them into realizing what occurred. There are a variety of ways to run a debriefing session. Some of the options include:

- Individual reporting;
- Small group discussion and reports;
- Large group question-and-answer format;
- Surveys and polling, using show of hands, flip-chart tallying, and so forth;
- Public opinion polls, obtaining as many different answers to each question as possible;
- One-on-one participant interviews and reports;
- Panel or round-table discussions; or
- Whips (quick free-association go-arounds).

The facilitator should concentrate on those questions that are relevant to the main topic of the session. Questions are provided with each activity, to guide participants in seeing the relevance of the event within the context of the objectives. These questions are by no means inclusive, and the facilitator should feel free to add others. In addition, feedback during the debriefing session may lead to other areas of discussion not specifically included here. This is especially true when "mistakes" have occurred during the actual event that may lead to new insights. For example, a group may devise a structure, build it, then ultimately have it collapse. A discussion can ensue as to why the structure did not last: Was it poor design? Ineffective use of materials? Unresolved conflict in the group? Limited participation by individuals? or What?

Summary

Games can be one of the most innovative and enjoyable parts of any training course. They stimulate discussion and learning and help illustrate, emphasize, or summarize a point in a very effective way. Because of their flexible structure, games help meet a variety of learning styles and can be used to explore a wide range of training topics.

In reality, experiential, hands-on learning exercises are not just fun and games. They encompass an audience-friendly approach that increases attention levels, keeps participants alert and productive, and boosts retention of information. Training games can be just the right vehicle to motivate participants to become actively involved in learning. And when learning becomes enjoyable, people develop the desire to comprehend even more.

All Together Now! is the third book in what can be viewed as the "Together Series." Like its predecessors, *Getting Together* and *Working Together*, it is a compilation of games that emphasize skills underlying the team spirit of group interactions. These activities give participants opportunities to explore the many facets of teamwork in an entertaining yet challenging way.

Learning can be FUN—seriously!

Exhibit I.2. Topics and Related Activities

Topic	Activities
Change	1, 2, 17, 20, 27, 29, 30, 40, 42, 51, 56, 59
Communication	4, 7, 8, 9, 10, 11, 12, 15, 18, 19, 26, 31, 35, 36, 41, 42, 43, 44, 46, 48, 49, 50, 51, 53, 54, 55, 59
Conflict Management	1, 7, 15, 19, 21, 22, 23, 28, 29, 30, 31, 45, 50, 53, 54, 56, 58, 59, 60
Creativity	3, 4, 6, 10, 12, 16, 17, 26, 35, 41, 46, 48, 49, 52
Decision Making	1, 2, 9, 13, 20, 21, 22, 24, 25, 26, 29, 31, 37, 38, 39, 40, 45, 50, 54, 57, 58
Diversity	7, 8, 10, 12, 14, 16, 21, 26, 31, 34, 37, 41, 45, 46, 47, 49, 55
Goal Setting	2, 3, 5, 18, 20, 32, 33, 39, 47
Icebreaker	5, 7, 8, 13, 14, 16, 18, 28, 37, 47, 48, 54, 55
Leadership	1, 17, 22, 30, 32, 36, 38, 42, 43, 52, 57
Negotiation	15, 19, 23, 24, 25, 31, 45, 53, 56, 59, 60
Perception	4, 5, 7, 9, 10, 12, 13, 14, 16, 17, 19, 25, 31, 32, 34, 35, 38, 41, 42, 44, 46, 48, 49, 50, 51, 55
Planning	1, 2, 6, 11, 13, 22, 24, 28, 29, 36, 39, 40, 47, 52, 56, 58
Problem Solving	3, 9, 11, 12, 13, 17, 22, 23, 24, 25, 26, 27, 29, 30, 32, 33, 35, 39, 40, 43, 44, 51, 54, 56, 57, 58
Resource Use	2, 6, 15, 23, 39, 52, 53, 56
Team Dynamics	1, 3, 4, 6, 7, 9, 10, 11, 13, 15, 16, 18, 20, 21, 22, 23, 24, 27, 28, 30, 31, 32, 33, 34, 35, 36, 37, 40, 41, 45, 46, 47, 49, 51, 52, 53, 56, 57, 59, 60

Activity Topics

Each activity in this book relates to one or more fundamental concept area in interpersonal and organizational behavior defined earlier in Exhibit I.1. Exhibit I.2 shows the topics and the numbers of corresponding activities that focus on the topic.

Activities

Added Value

Objective

To accumulate the most points by strategically collecting card values.

Applications

- Change
- Conflict Management
- Decision Making
- Leadership
- Planning
- Team Dynamics

Group Size

Six to forty participants, who will work in teams of two or three members each. A minimum of three teams is required.

Time Required

Twenty to thirty minutes.

Materials

One copy of the Added Value Tally Sheet, a pencil, one set of Added Value Cards, an envelope, and three counters in differing colors for each set of three teams; scissors.

Preparation

Duplicate two copies of the Added Value Cards sheet on card stock for each set of teams, then cut into separate cards. Place each set of forty-eight cards in an envelope.

Process

1. Instruct the participants to form teams of two or three members each. Have three teams form a set, seated at a common table. Each set is to select one player to score the game and oversee adherence to the rules; this player also will be a participating member of his or her team during its turn at play.

2. Distribute one copy of the Added Value Tally Sheet, a pencil, and one envelope of Added Value Cards to each set. Direct the scorer from each set to shuffle the forty-eight cards, then randomly arrange them face up in a 7 x 7 grid, leaving a blank space in the middle at the intersection of the fourth row and fourth column. Provide each team in the set with a different colored counter, all of which are to be placed in the blank space to start.

3. Explain that each team within the set will alternate, taking turns to move its counter in any one direction (horizontally, vertically, or diagonally) to any card *whose face value equals its distance from the previous position.* For example, if the counter moves from a "3" card, the team player counts three in any *one direction* to land on the new position. This card will determine the number of spaces that team will move on its *next* turn. Each time a team lands on a card, that card is turned face down and the team earns points equal to that card's face value. Face-down cards are to be counted when moving the counter. The first move can be made to any surrounding card, with the next move counted from that position. The scorer will keep a running tally of each team's score. The object of the game is for each team to accumulate as many points as possible. The game is over when no legal moves remain for any of the teams.

4. Answer any questions about the instructions. Signal for the activity to begin. After everyone has completed the game, determine which team was the winner within each set.

Discussion

- What strategic approach did your team take at the beginning of the game?
- As the opposing teams made their moves, how did your team adjust its strategy?
- How do unexpected changes impact strategic planning in the workplace?
- Was there equal participation in your teams' decision-making process?
- How were differences of opinion handled?
- How did a sense of competition affect your interaction with members of the opposing teams in your set?
- How might the role of the scorer take on leadership dimensions?

Added Value Cards

1	2	3	4
1	2	3	4
1	2	3	4
1	2	3	4
1	2	3	4
1	2	3	4

Added Value Tally Sheet

Directions to the Scorer: Write the color of the counter for each team at the top of the columns. Keep a running tally of each team's score throughout the game. Each time a team lands on a card, that card is turned face down, and the team earns points equal to the card's face value.

Rules: A counter may be moved in any one direction (horizontally, vertically, or diagonally) to any card *whose face value equals its distance from the previous position.* For example, if the counter moves from a "3" card, the team player counts three in any *one direction* to land on the new position. This card determines the number of spaces that team will move on its *next* turn. Face-down cards are to be counted when moving the counter. The first move can be made to any surrounding card, with the next move counted from that position. The game is over when no legal moves remain for any of the teams.

Team	Team	Team

Bidding Wars

Objective

To obtain the highest score by strategically bidding for numbered tiles.

Applications

- Change
- Decision Making
- Goal Setting
- Planning
- Resource Use

Group Size

Six to twenty participants, who will work in teams of three to four members each. A minimum of two teams is required.

Time Required

Twenty to thirty minutes.

Materials

One set of Bidding Wars Cards in an envelope for each team; one set of Bidding Wars Tiles; scissors; flip chart and felt-tipped marker; stopwatch.

Preparation

Duplicate the Bidding Wars Tiles and Bidding Wars Cards on card stock. Cut the sheets into separate pieces, keeping each set separate. Place each set of cards in an envelope. Shuffle the tiles and keep them face down. Prepare a flip chart with the following information:

- POSITIVE numbers are won by the HIGHEST bidding card.
- NEGATIVE numbers are won by the LOWEST bidding card.
- If two or more winning bids are equal, next highest (or next lowest) bid wins.
- If all bids are the same, no one wins the tile. Next winning bid receives both tiles.

Process

1. Instruct the participants to form teams of three or four members each.

2. Explain that the teams will be competing against each other in a "bidding war" to win *tiles* with numbers from –5 to +10 (no zero). Each tile counts as its face value. The winner of the tournament is the team with the most tile points at the end.

3. Distribute one envelope containing Bidding War Cards to each team.

4. Explain that each one of the fifteen cards in the set may be used once only by the team. The facilitator will display one tile at a time and teams will have thirty seconds in which to select cards representing their bids. At a signal, all the teams will reveal their bids simultaneously. Referring to the prepared flip chart, review the rules for the winning bids:

   - POSITIVE number tiles are won by the HIGHEST bidding card.
   - NEGATIVE number tiles are won by the LOWEST bidding card.
   - If two or more winning bids are the same, they cancel each other out. The team with the next highest (or next lowest) bid wins the tile.
   - If all bids are the same, no one wins the tile. The next tile is revealed and the team winning this bid receives both tiles.

5. Using the face-down pile of Bidding Wars Tiles, turn up the first tile and show it to the teams. Announce that they will have thirty seconds in which to discuss the bid to be placed.

6. Time the discussion, then signal for the teams to display their bids. Determine the winning bid according to the rules above. Give the tile to the appropriate team, and collect all the bidding cards for that round. Turn up the next tile and repeat this process until all tiles have been awarded.

7. Instruct the teams to count the tiles in their possession for a final score. Remind participants that the tiles count at face value. Determine the highest score and announce the winning team.

Discussion

- Did your team do as well as you thought it would? Why or why not?
- Because you could use each bidding card only once, how did your team determine the best use of this resource?
- How did your team decide on what bid to make?
- How did time pressure (that is, the thirty-second discussion period) affect the planning and decision-making process?
- As your team won or lost during the bidding, how effectively did your team adjust its strategy to the changing conditions?
- How does this activity relate to goal setting and planning in the work environment?

Bidding Wars Tiles

–5	–4	–3
–2	–1	1
2	3	4
5	6	7
8	9	10

Bidding Wars Cards

1	2	3
4	5	6
7	8	9
10	11	12
13	14	15

Bridging the Gap

Objective

To complete a series of words by using the appropriate connecting words.

Applications

- Creativity
- Goal Setting
- Problem Solving
- Team Dynamics

Group Size

Five to fifty participants, who will work in teams of three to five members each.

Time Required

Twenty minutes.

Materials

One copy of the Bridging the Gap Worksheet and a pencil for each participant; flip chart and felt-tipped marker; clock or timer.

Preparation

None.

Process

1. Instruct participants to form teams of three to five members each.

2. Distribute one copy of the Bridging the Gap Worksheet and a pencil to each participant.

3. Explain that the goal of this activity is to find the appropriate word for each blank that connects it with the preceding word, as well as with the word that follows, to make a compound word or well-known, two-word phrase. Refer to the example at the top of the worksheet: *light house boat*. Explain that "light" connects to "house" for "lighthouse" and that "house" connects to "boat" for "houseboat." Each line, when the blanks are filled in, results in an interconnected series of words. Announce that teams will have a total of ten minutes to complete their worksheets.

4. Writing their answers on a flip-chart sheet, have teams predict how many of the ten possible answers they will be able to complete in the set time period.

5. Signal for the activity to begin. Time the discussion for ten minutes, giving a two-minute warning; then stop the activity.

6. Review each word series, one line at a time, by first obtaining answers from the teams, then revealing the correct word for each blank space, according to the information given below.

Answers:

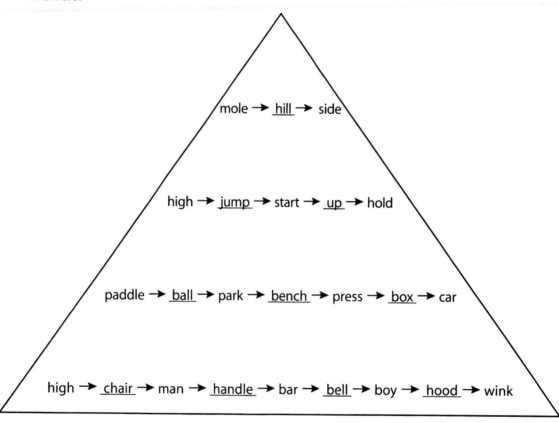

7. Have each team report back its correct number of answers and compare with its recorded goal on the flip-chart sheet.

Discussion

- How close did your team come to its predicted results?
- What considerations did you take into account when setting your goal?
- How might this game be compared with the process of creative problem solving?
- In what ways did working as a group help or hinder your completion of this exercise?

Bridging the Gap Worksheet

Directions: Find the appropriate word for each blank that connects with the preceding word as well as with the word that follows. For example:

light → <u>house</u> → boat

"Light" connects to "house" for "lighthouse," then "house" connects to "boat" for "houseboat." Each line below will result in an interconnected series of words when all the blanks have been filled. You will have ten minutes to complete this worksheet.

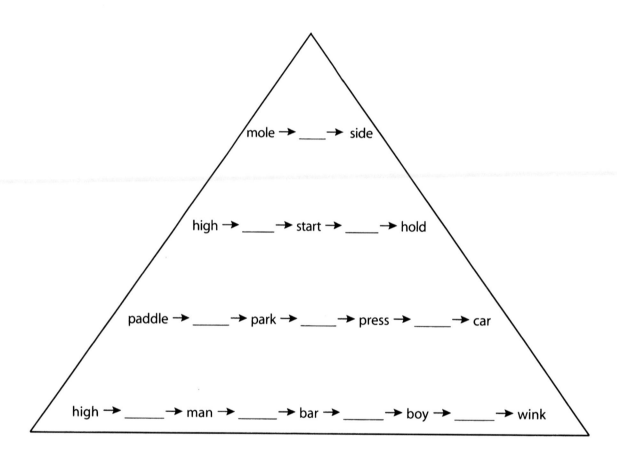

mole → ＿＿＿ → side

high → ＿＿＿ → start → ＿＿＿ → hold

paddle → ＿＿＿ → park → ＿＿＿ → press → ＿＿＿ → car

high → ＿＿＿ → man → ＿＿＿ → bar → ＿＿＿ → boy → ＿＿＿ → wink

By All Accounts

Objective

To relate a group story based on individually assigned objects.

Applications

- Communication
- Creativity
- Perception
- Team Dynamics

Group Size

Eight to thirty participants, who will work in teams of eight to ten members each.

Time Required

Ten to twenty minutes.

Materials

One paper lunch bag for each participant; one item for each participant from a variety of small, familiar objects (for example, comb, string, glove, cup, matches, mirror, button, feather, light bulb, spoon, nickel, shoelace, ruler, scissors, pen, eraser, band-aid, rubber band, sock, ball, and so on).

Preparation

Place one object in each paper lunch bag, then fold the top of the bag several times to close it. *Note:* It is recommended that a variety of objects be used, but it is acceptable to have similar or even identical objects when more than one team participates, providing these items are distributed to different groups.

Process

1. Instruct the participants to form teams of approximately eight to ten members each. Direct each group to sit in a circle in a separate location. Select one person in each team to act as leader.

2. Distribute one prepared paper bag to each participant, announcing that the bags are to remain closed until further instruction.

3. Explain that each team, in turn, will be telling an original story, using the objects inside the bags to help relate the tale. Each person will have a turn telling a part of the story using the prop in the bag in front of him or her. The story will proceed from person to person in a clockwise direction. Participants should speak for just a few sentences when it is their turn. Emphasize that each new speaker should refrain from starting the sentence with the word "and" in order to allow for discrete ideas to form. Remind the participants that it is important for members of a team to work together to ensure that the overall story makes sense.

4. Select one team and direct the participants to open their bags and remove the individual items. Designate one person to begin the story and signal for the team to start.

5. When the first team has completed its story, repeat the process described in Step 4 for the second group, then the third group, as appropriate. Explain that the story is to begin anew for each group.

Variation

Have participants tell a story using the props in a symbolic sense. For example, a flashlight might indicate "energy" or string might mean "rules that bind."

Discussion

- How difficult was this task? Why?
- In what ways did individual input contribute to the team effort?
- What factors played a role in helping a team's story to make sense?
- Why was active listening such a critical component?
- How did perception play a role in this activity?
- Were some parts of the story more creative than others? Give some examples and explain why.

Character Reference

Objective

To list characters with whom individuals identify as being most or least like themselves.

Applications

- Goal Setting
- Icebreaker
- Perception

Group Size

Four to fifty participants, who will work in teams of four or five members each.

Time Required

Twenty to thirty minutes.

Materials

One copy of the Character Reference Worksheet and a pencil for each participant; clock or timer.

Preparation

None.

Process

1. Distribute one copy of the Character Reference Worksheet and a pencil to each participant.

2. Referring to the worksheet, explain that each participant is to list three different character names: one you would *most like to be,* one you would *least like to be,* and the one who is *most like you.* The name of the person may be chosen from real life, fiction, the news, movies, literature, cartoons, history, or whatever else fits. Remind participants that they should also include the reason why they chose a particular character. Announce that participants will have five minutes to complete this task.

3. Signal for individuals to begin. Time the activity for five minutes, then stop work when time expires.

4. Instruct the participants to form teams of four or five members each.

5. Explain that participants are to take turns sharing their lists with their teammates, explaining why the characters were chosen. After all the team members have shared this information, they should examine the combined lists for similarities and differences. Announce that teams will have fifteen minutes for group discussion.

6. Signal for the discussion to begin. Time the activity for fifteen minutes, giving a five-minute warning; then stop the teams when time expires.

7. Direct the participants to turn their worksheets over. Explain that each individual is to write one personal goal statement that exemplifies an admirable trait of his or her role model character ("Most like to be"). The statement should include a specific action that the participant will take in order to help incorporate the characteristic into his or her life. Allow several minutes for this task to be completed.

Discussion

- What kind of characters were mentioned most often in your group for most like to be? Least like to be? Most like you?

- In what ways did individuals' perceptions of the characters differ?

- What were some of the reasons given for those characters you would most like to be?

- How do role models influence personal expectations and goals?

Character Reference Worksheet

The character I would *most like to be* is:

because

The character I would *most like to be* is:

because

The character I would *most like to be* is:

because

Chip Ship

Objective

To package a potato chip in a way that it will not break under the pressure of a weight test.

Applications

- Creativity
- Planning
- Problem Solving
- Resource Use
- Team Dynamics

Group Size

Four to thirty participants, who will work in teams of three or four members each.

Time Required

Thirty to forty minutes.

Materials

One Pringles® potato chip for each team (as they are equal in size and strength); tape; a variety of packaging materials, such as cotton, Styrofoam® boxes, or egg cartons, to be shared by all teams; dictionary; ruler; clock or timer.

Preparation

Place the tape and the packaging materials on a table centrally located to all teams.

Process

1. Instruct the participants to form teams of three or four members each.

2. Distribute one potato chip to each team.

3. Referring to the table containing the packing supplies, explain that the goal for each team is to make a package for shipping its potato chip with no breakage. All teams must share the resources supplied. The package must be able to pass the Chip Ship Test: The package will be shaken, then a dictionary will be held six inches over the package and dropped on it. Announce that teams will have twenty minutes to complete the project.

4. Signal for group work to begin. Time the activity for twenty minutes, giving a two-minute warning; then stop the activity when time expires.

5. Using the ruler and book, conduct the Chip Ship Test on each team's package. Check to see whether each chip broke.

Discussion

- How did your team approach its assignment?
- If your chip broke, how could your team have packed it better?
- What impact did the sharing of resources have on your team's completion of the project?
- How well did team members work together on this activity?

Choice Cuts

Objective

To examine individual personality by selecting representative terms from word pairs.

Applications

- Communication
- Conflict Management
- Diversity
- Icebreaker
- Perception
- Team Dynamics

Group Size

Five to fifty participants, who will work in teams of four to five members each.

Time Required

Thirty to forty minutes.

Materials

One Choice Cuts Worksheet and a pencil for each participant; one Choice Cuts Tally Sheet for each team; flip chart and felt-tipped marker; clock or timer.

Preparation

Prepare a flip-chart sheet with the ten word pairs, allowing enough space beneath each to keep a tally.

Process

1. Begin with a discussion about the wide range of differences in items available to us and the variety of choices that each of us has to make every day. Ask the participants for some other examples of choices we must make, both simple and complex. Next, introduce the topic of differences that are specific to individuals—likes, dislikes, wants, needs, personalities, and so on. Say that individual personality and behavioral style result from a combination of things unique to each of us, such as experiences, upbringing, education, beliefs, value systems, and so forth.

2. Explain that the participants will participate in an activity that will give them an opportunity to express their individuality. Distribute one copy of the Choice Cuts Worksheet and a pencil to each participant.

3. Explain that, for each pair of words presented on the worksheet, each participant is to circle the *one word* that is most representative of his or her personality and to write the reason why. Point out that participants should be as explicit as possible in stating their reasons. Announce that they will have five minutes in which to complete the task.

4. Signal for the activity to begin. Time the process for five minutes, then stop the activity.

5. Instruct the participants to form teams of four or five members each. Have each team select a member to be the team recorder.

6. Distribute one copy of the Choice Cuts Tally Sheet to each team. Direct the teams to discuss their individual choices and reasons. The team recorder should complete the Tally Sheet by circling the term from each word pair that represents the *majority of the group members*. Individual reasons for each choice should also be recorded. Announce that teams will have fifteen minutes to complete the task.

7. Signal for the discussion to begin. Time the activity for fifteen minutes, giving a five-minute warning; then stop the discussion.

8. Using the prepared flip chart, place a mark under the appropriate "majority choice" for each word pair as each team makes its report.

Discussion

- Were the reasons individuals gave for their choices similar? What are some examples?
- How does this wide range of perceptions affect interpersonal relationships?
- How can a wide range of perceptions affect communication processes?
- How can diverse personalities (or ideas) enhance a team process?
- How do similarities among team members strengthen group cohesion?

Choice Cuts Worksheet

Directions: For each word pair, circle the one term that you feel best represents something characteristic of your personality and then write the reason why.

Choice	Reasons
Regular OR Decaf	
Paper OR Plastic	
Sheer OR Opaque	
Heavy OR Light	
Automatic OR Manual	
Bottle OR Can	
Bird OR Bee	
Top OR Bottom	
Plain OR Fancy	
Circle OR Square	

Choice Cuts Tally Sheet

Team Recorder: For each word pair presented, circle the one term that represents the choice for the majority of team members and write examples of the reasons why.

Choice	Reasons
Regular OR Decaf	
Paper OR Plastic	
Sheer OR Opaque	
Heavy OR Light	
Automatic OR Manual	
Bottle OR Can	
Bird OR Bee	
Top OR Bottom	
Plain OR Fancy	
Circle OR Square	

Class Act

Objective

To group individuals together according to similarities and learn new things about one another in the process.

Applications

- Communication
- Diversity
- Icebreaker

Group Size

An unlimited number of participants.

Time Required

Ten to fifteen minutes.

Materials

List of classifications or categories to announce. (You may wish to use some of the following suggestions or create your own, incorporating topics from a specific content area, such as color of eyes, number of siblings, make of car, favorite flavor of ice cream, favorite kind of music, favorite TV show, or month of birth.)

Preparation

None.

Process

1. Direct the participants to gather in a central location.

2. Explain that the object of the activity is to form groups that are similar, according to the classifications that you give. Each time a new order is given, participants are to form new groups according to the stated category.

3. Announce one classification or category from the prepared list. Allow a sufficient amount of time for groups to form according to the specification.

4. Announce a new category and continue with this procedure for several more times before ending the activity.

Variation

Have participants form groups that contain members of all different qualifications according to the category announced; for example, if eye color is the category, a group may be composed of one person each with blue eyes, green eyes, and brown eyes.

Discussion

- Which categories made it more difficult to find partners? Why?
- How did you feel about obtaining the appropriate information in order to group together?
- How willing were others to offer the necessary information?
- Why was open communication important for conducting this activity?
- (Variation): How do diverse collections of people benefit from one another?

Comics Counseling

Objective

To solve a comic character's problem by examining alternative solutions.

Applications

- Communication
- Decision Making
- Perception
- Problem Solving
- Team Dynamics

Group Size

Five to thirty participants, who will work in teams of three to five members each.

Time Required

Thirty minutes.

Materials

One *Comics* section of a newspaper, one copy of the Comics Counseling Worksheet, and one pencil for each team; clock or timer.

Preparation

Using several newspapers, obtain one *Comics* section for each participating team.

Process

1. Instruct the participants to form teams of three to five members each. Have each team select one person to record the group's work.

2. Distribute one copy of the Comics Counseling Worksheet, a pencil, and one *Comics* section of a newspaper to each participating team.

3. Using the newspaper as a source, direct each team to locate a character who has a problem or who is facing a dilemma. Explain that each team will have to solve the character's problem using the following process: (1) understand and state the problem; (2) list a variety of ways in which to solve the problem; and (3) choose the best solution. The team recorder will make notes on the discussion using the worksheet provided. Announce that the teams will have fifteen minutes to complete the task.

4. Signal for the activity to begin. Time the discussion for fifteen minutes, giving a five-minute warning; then stop the group work when time expires.

5. Gather together the whole group and have each team, in turn, deliver a report on its discussion of the three topics assigned.

Variation

Select one comic strip and duplicate a copy for each team. Have all the teams use the same character to complete the assigned steps.

Discussion

- How does this activity relate to problem solving in general?
- How did the wording of the problem statement affect your approach to finding solutions?
- What limited your ability to find an appropriate solution?
- What could you have done to improve your problem-solving technique?

Comics Counseling Worksheet

Problem Statement:

Alternative Solutions:

Chosen Solution:

Communication
Connection

Objective

To use gestures as a means of communication, subject to personal interpretation.

Applications

- Communication
- Creativity
- Diversity
- Perception
- Team Dynamics

Group Size

Six to fifty participants, who will work in teams of three to five members each. A minimum of three teams is required.

Time Required

Thirty minutes.

Materials

One copy of the Communication Connection Worksheet and a pencil for each team; clock or timer.

Preparation

None.

Process

1. Instruct the participants to form teams of three to five participants each, seated in separate locations.

2. Distribute one copy of the Communication Connection Worksheet and a pencil to each team.

3. Explain that, depending on where you are in the world, body language and common gestures mean entirely different things. What is funny or friendly in one culture may be rude or even vulgar in another. A gesture meant to comfort may be anxiety-provoking or antagonistic. For example, nodding the head slightly to signify "yes" is not a universal gesture. In parts of Greece, Turkey, and other countries in the Middle East, it means "no." The way people wave "good-bye" in the United States is the same way some Middle Eastern cultures indicate "come here." Say that this activity will provide participants with a chance to explore body language as a means of communication.

4. Announce that each group will have five minutes in which to make up some entirely new gestures and describe what each means on the worksheet provided. These gestures will become their only means of communication with other teams later in the activity.

5. Signal for the discussion to begin; call time after five minutes.

6. Explain that now the entire group will participate in a universal gathering in which each team will use gestures as the sole means of communication with the other teams. Spoken language may not be used. Participants are to try to discover the meaning of the gestures as they interact with one another.

7. Signal for the activity to begin. Stop the group after approximately ten minutes and instruct participants to return to their original teams.

8. Have each team demonstrate its gestures to the larger group. Obtain feedback on the possible meaning of each gesture from other teams before having the originating team describe the actual meaning.

Discussion

- How did your team determine the content of its communication with other teams?
- What factors did your team take into account in order to create its gestures?
- How difficult was it to interpret the gestures of others during the gathering?
- What hindered the process? What helped?
- What similarities did you find among the gestures? Differences?
- How does the perception of body language influence personal interactions?

Communication Connection Worksheet

Gesture	Meaning

Construction Sight

Objective

To construct an object from building materials according to written instructions.

Applications

- Communication
- Planning
- Problem Solving
- Team Dynamics

Group Size

Eight to twenty-four participants, who will work in teams of four to six members each. A minimum of two teams is required.

Time Required

Thirty minutes.

Materials

Two identical sets of building materials (Legos® Tinkertoys® Lincoln Logs® blocks, or toothpicks and gumdrops), two plastic bags, one large shopping bag with handles, one sheet of paper, and a pencil for each team; clock or timer.

Preparation

For each team, place each of the two identical building sets in a separate plastic bag; then put both bags into a large shopping bag. *Note:* It is important that the second set of materials be identical to the first one in every way, including number, size, shape, and color. However, one team may have a different type of material from another team.

Process

1. Instruct the participants to form teams of four to six members each. Each team should be located at a table in a separate area that allows for privacy.

2. Distribute one shopping bag of building materials to each team.

3. Explain that each team is to remove one set of materials from the bag, leaving the other set inside. Using the building materials, teams will have five minutes in which to construct something, such as a space station, home, playground, or car. Emphasize that the construction should be kept hidden from the other teams and that the shopping bag can be used to shield the object from view. Encourage the teams to use as many of the items as possible.

4. Signal for the construction to begin, then call time after five minutes. Tell the teams that they are no longer allowed to touch the constructed object.

5. Distribute one sheet of paper and a pencil to each team. Explain that each team is to describe its object as fully as possible in words—clearly enough so that someone can replicate the construction identically from just the written description. No symbols or drawings may be used. Teams will have ten minutes to complete this portion of the task.

6. Signal for work to begin. Time the activity for ten minutes, giving a five-minute and a two-minute warning; then signal for teams to stop when time expires.

7. Direct the teams to take the second set of building materials out of the shopping bag and place it beside the constructed piece. Next, have each team cover its object with the shopping bag and place the written description of the construction next to the building materials.

8. Instruct each team to trade places with another team. Using the building materials and the written instructions for construction, each team will have five minutes in which to make an identical object.

9. Signal for work to begin. Time the activity for five minutes, giving a two-minute warning; then signal for teams to stop when time expires.

10. Direct each team to remove the shopping bag from the original structure, comparing the second construction to the first one.

Discussion

- How difficult was this challenge? Why?
- If you encountered incomplete or unclear information in the construction notes, how did your team solve the problem?

- What interpretations, if any, turned out to be correct? Incorrect?
- In what ways could the written instructions you received have been improved?
- Was there balanced participation among team members during the activity? Why or why not?
- What specific roles, if any, emerged for individual team members?

Creative License

Objective

To decode, then create license plates that reflect different types of individuals.

Applications

- Communication
- Creativity
- Diversity
- Perception
- Problem Solving

Group Size

Six to thirty participants, who will work in teams of three to five members each.

Time Required

Thirty to forty minutes.

Materials

One copy of the Creative License Worksheet and a pencil for each participant; five 5″ x 8″ index cards and a felt-tipped marker for each team; flip chart and felt-tipped marker; clock or timer.

Preparation

Create a flip-chart sheet that lists the following information:

> Using no more than seven letters or numbers, create a license plate that describes three of the following:
>
> > A basketball player
> >
> > A medical student
> >
> > An Olympic athlete
> >
> > A parent
> >
> > A scuba diver

Process

1. Distribute one copy of the Creative License Worksheet and a pencil to each participant.

2. Referring to the worksheet, explain that individuals will attempt to decode each of the personalized license plates presented, then write a description of the type of person it might fit. Announce that participants will have five minutes to complete this task.

3. Signal for individual work to begin. Time the activity; then stop participants when time expires.

4. Review the decoded answers through participant feedback, checking the information against the answers below. Then solicit individual responses about the type of person each would fit.

   Answers:

(1) EDUCATE	(4) FOREST LOVER
(2) WEIGHT WATCHER	(5) TENNIS ANYONE
(3) BEFORE YOU LEAP	

5. Instruct the participants to form teams of three to five members each. Distribute five index cards and a felt-tipped marker to each team.

6. Referring to the prepared flip chart, explain that each team will now design its own license plates from at least three of the five descriptions listed. These licenses are to use no more than seven letters or numbers each. Announce that teams will have fifteen minutes to complete the task. Teams that complete the initial three before time expires should continue working on the additional two descriptions.

7. Signal for group work to begin. Time the activity for fifteen minutes, giving a five-minute warning; then stop the teams when time expires.

8. Have the teams take turns presenting their license plates and then asking the group as a whole to decode each one.

Discussion

- In what ways did creativity play a role in this activity?
- How difficult was it to communicate a message through the license plates?
- How difficult was this task overall? Why?
- How might an individual's perception of others affect his or her viewpoint?
- How can we combine the personal preferences (likes and dislikes) of individuals to make a more effective working environment?

Creative License Worksheet

Directions: Decode each of the personalized license plates below, then write a description of the type of person it might fit.

1.  ED U K8

2.  W8WACHR

3. 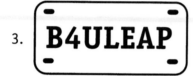 B4ULEAP

4.  4STLUVR

5. 10S NE1

Dicey Digits

Objective

To cover number squares determined through individual rolls of the dice.

Applications

- Decision Making
- Icebreaker
- Perception
- Planning
- Problem Solving
- Team Dynamics

Group Size

Six to fifty participants, who will work in teams of two or three members each. A minimum of three teams is required.

Time Required

Fifteen to thirty minutes.

Materials

One copy each of the Dicey Digits Game Cards 1, 2, and 3, one pair of dice, and a felt-tipped marker for each set of three teams.

Preparation

Consider the time available and decide beforehand whether the winner will be the first team in each set to cover one complete line, two lines, or the whole card.

Process

1. Instruct the participants to form teams of two or three members each. Have three teams form a set, located in a common area.

2. Distribute the Dicey Digits Game Cards 1, 2, and 3 to each set of three teams, giving a different card to each team. Provide one pair of dice and a felt-tipped marker for each set.

3. Explain that this game is similar to Bingo, except that it is played with dice. Each team has a different card, and the object is to cover the numbers on its card more quickly than the other teams in the set. Teams will alternate turns, with the team holding Game Card 1 going first.

4. Explain the rules of play as follows:

   The team player throws the dice and notes the resulting numbers. The figures can be used in a variety of ways to suit pertinent requirements. The numbers on the dice can be *added*, *subtracted*, or used as *separate* figures in a number combination. A double number is a "wild card."

   Give the following example:

   A roll of 2 and 4 might be used as 6 (added), as 2 (subtracted), or as separate figures to provide 24 or 42 (combined). A double number (two 1's, two 2's, etc.) is a "wild card" and can be used to cover any number on the card. The number to use in each case will be chosen by the team according to what is available on its Game Card. The team will use the felt-tipped marker to place a large "X" on the desired number, then pass the dice and marker to the next team. If no corresponding number is available on the card, the turn is forfeited.

5. Announce the predetermined method of winning (see Preparation), then signal for the game to begin. Stop the activity after each set has declared a winning team.

Variation

Provide each team within the set with a copy of the *same* Game Card. This still allows only one team within each set to win, because each team throws the dice to determine the numbers that score on that team's card only.

Discussion

- What planning strategy did your team use to approach the task?
- As the game progressed, did your team need to adjust its strategy? Why or why not?
- What factors affected your ability to eliminate numbers?

- Because each team had a different Game Card, what was your perception of the equality of play?
- How did this affect your team's view of the opposing teams? *Note:* You can now explain that the Game Cards were prepared using number combinations that gave each team an equal chance.
- How well did team members work together to make decisions?

Dicey Digits Game Card 1

1	14	26
6	15	31
8	16	32
10	23	34
12	24	35

Dicey Digits Game Card 2

2	15	26
5	16	31
8	21	34
10	23	35
12	24	36

Dicey Digits Game Card 3

3	15	31
7	21	32
8	23	33
10	24	35
13	25	36

Drawing on Experience

Objective

To see how different people assign unique meanings to information collected from the same experience.

Applications

- Diversity
- Icebreaker
- Perception

Group Size

Six to thirty participants, who will work in teams of four to six members each.

Time Required

Fifteen minutes.

Materials

One object with distinct shape and texture (for example, a cheese grater, vase, stuffed animal, or woven basket) for each team; one sheet of paper and a pencil for each participant; one blindfold for each participant (optional).

Preparation

None.

Process

1. Instruct the participants to form teams of four to six members each. Direct the members of each team to form a line and close their eyes. Announce that everyone's eyes should remain closed until you tell them to open them. (Blindfolds are optional.)

2. Explain that each team will receive an object that has a very distinct shape and texture. Each member of the team will have an opportunity to hold the object long enough to collect some information before passing it on to the next person.

3. Provide the first person in line for each team with an object and direct him or her to hold the object for a brief period of time, then to pass it on to the next person in line, until each person has had an opportunity to hold the object. Remind participants to keep their eyes closed.

4. Collect the object from each team, noting which one was given to which team. Place the objects out of sight; then direct participants to open their eyes.

5. Distribute one sheet of paper and a pencil to each person. Instruct the participants, working alone, to draw a picture of what they think the object looks like.

6. Have each team compare the drawings of its individual members, noting similarities and differences among the drawings.

7. Return the appropriate object to each team and have members compare the drawings with the actual object.

Discussion

- What past experiences influenced your depiction of the object?
- In what ways do our past experiences and perceptions affect our views of the "real" world?
- How does having a variety of different views benefit a team? Hinder it?

Eternal Triangles

Objective

To acquire completed playing cards by bartering for necessary pieces.

Applications

- Communication
- Conflict Management
- Negotiation
- Resource Use
- Team Dynamics

Group Size

Nine to fifty participants, who will work in teams of three to five members each. A minimum of three teams is required. The Variation allows participation as individuals, rather than as teams, with a maximum of twenty participants.

Time Required

Twenty to thirty minutes.

Materials

One envelope for each team (or one for each participant if using the Variation); one deck of playing cards; scissors; clock or timer.

Preparation

Cut each individual playing card into four triangular-shaped pieces. To do this, first cut the card in half diagonally to form two large triangles. Next, hold both pieces together and cut diagonally again to create four triangular pieces. (See the diagram below.) Mix all the card pieces thoroughly, then randomly place them into the envelopes in relatively equal amounts.

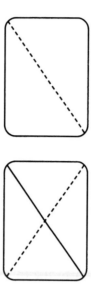

Process

1. Instruct the participants to form teams of three to five members each.

2. Distribute one envelope to each team. Explain that the envelopes contain pieces of individual playing cards that have been cut into four pieces. The object now is for each team to form as many complete cards as possible by first examining the cards in the envelope and forming complete or nearly complete sets. Then, upon a signal, teams will have ten minutes in which to barter with other teams for missing segments.

3. Allow a few minutes for groups to examine their card pieces for matches, then ask for everyone's attention. Tell the groups that they will now be allowed to barter with other groups for missing pieces that are needed to complete the cards. Announce that the teams will have ten minutes to complete the bartering process.

4. Signal for the activity to begin. Time the process for ten minutes, giving a two-minute warning; then stop the activity. Allow members of each team a few more minutes to reassemble and complete the card matches.

5. Determine which team has the most completed cards (all four triangles per whole card).

Variation

For smaller groups, prepare one envelope for each participant and conduct the bartering process individually, rather than in teams.

Discussion

- How willing were other teams (individuals) to trade card pieces?
- What processes were used to conduct the bartering? Were these processes effective?
- How would the process have been affected if the activity were conducted as individuals (teams)?
- What implications does what happened here have for the workplace?
- How does the need to share resources impact the workplace?

Exercising Your Strength

Objective

To explore individual and composite team strengths through representative objects.

Applications

- Creativity
- Diversity
- Icebreaker
- Perception
- Team Dynamics

Group Size

One or several groups of intact work teams of approximately five to twelve members each.

Time Required

Fifteen to twenty minutes.

Materials

A wide variety of common objects, such as rubber bands, paper clips, string, balls, cups, tape, boxes, or erasers, each in sufficient supply so that several participants could choose the same item; clock or timer.

Preparation

Display the objects on a table in a common area.

Process

1. Instruct the members of intact work teams to gather together, with each group located in a separate area of the room.

2. Referring to the table with the displayed objects, explain that each individual is to select one object that symbolizes his or her own personal strength as a member of the work team. Signal for the participants to make their selections.

3. After all members of the team have made their selections, explain that each person is to share briefly with the other members of his or her team how the object chosen represents a particular strength (for example, a rubber band may represent flexibility). Announce that teams will have five minutes to complete the task.

4. Signal for the teams to begin the activity. Time the discussion for five minutes, then stop the activity. Direct the members of each team to use all the selected objects to make a structural representation of the team's strengths in an integrated way. It should show what the individuals combined can give to the team and what will become the backbone of its success. *Note:* The structure may take the form of a horizontal or vertical sculpture, or merely a loosely connected series of objects. Announce that teams will have five minutes to complete this task.

5. Signal for the group work to begin. Time the activity for five minutes, then stop the teams when time expires.

6. Direct each team to report back, with individual team members describing the strength represented by their personal objects and how they were integrated into the team's final product.

Discussion

- Did the same object represent different things to various people? Why?
- Why is it important for individuals to recognize their personal strengths?
- How do various individual strengths assist the team as a whole?
- Why do teams need a variety of different kinds of skills and interests?

Flextime

Objective

To match words having creatively disguised relationships.

Applications

- Change
- Creativity
- Leadership
- Perception
- Problem Solving

Group Size

Six to thirty participants, who will work in teams of three to five members each. A minimum of two teams is required.

Time Required

Thirty minutes.

Materials

One copy of the Flextime Worksheet and a pencil for each participant; stopwatch; flip chart and felt-tipped marker.

Preparation

None.

Process

1. Instruct the participants to form teams of three to five members each. Provide each team with a separate designation (a letter, number, color, shape, or other distinguishable feature). Select one person from each team to be the leader.

2. Distribute one copy of the Flextime Worksheet and a pencil to each participant.

3. Referring to the worksheet, read aloud the directions at the top of the page. Explain that the team leader will be responsible for guiding the discussion and recording the final solutions for each group. When a team completes its worksheet, the leader is to stand and ask that the completion time be recorded on the flip chart. Teams are to continue working until all groups have completed the task. Explain that the first team to complete the puzzle *correctly* will be the winner.

4. Signal for the activity to begin and start the stopwatch. As each team leader stands, record the team designation and finish time on the flip chart. Continue timing and recording until all teams have finished. If not all teams have finished at the end of twenty minutes, stop the activity.

5. Direct the leader of the team that finished first to reveal each answer, checking for correctness using the Answers section below. If an answer is incorrect, ask other team leaders to respond with their answers until the correct one is revealed. Determine the winning team based on finish time and number of correct answers.

Answers:

(1) D (to-wed = engaged)

(2) G (awning = super-visor)

(3) I (back burner = rear-range)

(4) A (inside trading = organ transplants)

(5) H (dugout = under-stands)

(6) B (clan-king = chieftain)

(7) F (archery fan = bow-lover)

(8) E (blush = go-red)

(9) J (be-a-con = go to jail)

(10) C (run away = leg-it)

Discussion

- How difficult was this task? What made it difficult?
- How did time pressure impact your ability to solve this puzzle?
- Was the leader's role critical to the team's ability to perform this task? Why or why not?
- How does an individual's way of perceiving things affect his or her ability to solve problems?
- What are some things we can do to learn to look at things in new and different ways?
- Today's workplace is marked by rapid change. Why is it important to improve our mental flexibility to adapt to new situations and conditions?

Flextime Worksheet

Directions: The object of this puzzle is to match the ten items on the left with the ten on the right based on similar or related meanings. The relationships are disguised by the use of puns, double meanings, or altered spacing within the words. For example, "accost" can be matched with "electric bill" (AC cost).

Be creative! You'll need to keep your mind flexible in order to see some of the relationships!

_____ 1. towed	A. organ transplants
_____ 2. awning	B. chieftain
_____ 3. back burner	C. legit
_____ 4. inside trading	D. engaged
_____ 5. dugout	E. gored
_____ 6. clanking	F. bowl over
_____ 7. archery fan	G. supervisor
_____ 8. blush	H. understands
_____ 9. beacon	I. rearrange
_____ 10. run away	J. go to jail

Force Field

Objective

To escape as a team through an opening in an "electric force field."

Applications

- Communication
- Goal Setting
- Icebreaker
- Team Dynamics

Group Size

Ten to forty participants, who will work in teams of five to eight members each. A minimum of two teams is required.

Time Required

Twenty to forty-five minutes.

Materials

Two 25-foot (approximately) pieces of clothesline rope; masking tape; tape measure; one index card and a pencil for each team; flip chart and felt-tipped marker.

Preparation

Divide the room in half by taping (or tying) the two ropes from one side to the other, one approximately two feet and the other approximately five feet from the floor.

Process

1. Instruct the participants to form teams of five to eight members each, then provide each with a separate team designation. Direct all the teams to gather on one side of the suspended ropes.

2. Explain that the ropes represent an electric force field and that the groups will be trapped unless they are able to pass through the opening. All the members of a team will be required to hold hands as they work together to escape to the other side. Any player who accidentally touches either rope will be zapped with electricity. Due to their connection with the rest of the group, the entire team will die. The object is to move all of the team from one side to the other without being zapped. Emphasize that all the play will be done silently, as they are escaping in secret.

3. Signal for the first team to hold hands and then to move through the ropes. After all the members have passed through, direct the second team to go. Continue this process until all the teams have attempted to pass through the ropes once. If a member from any team touches either rope during the attempt, that team forfeits its turn.

4. After all teams have completed one attempt, explain that each team will have a second opportunity to pass through the electric force field. This time team members will be allowed to talk during the attempt, and each team will be allowed to determine the placement of the two ropes. The width between the ropes will become the score for the team, with each inch counting as one point. Once again, team members must hold hands and any team member touching either of the ropes will be zapped, with the team scoring zero. The team with the *lowest* score (excluding zero) will be the winner.

5. Distribute one index card and a pencil to each team. Direct each team to write its team designation and the height of the bottom rope and the top rope for its attempt on the card. Collect all the cards.

6. As each team takes its turn, adjust the bottom and top ropes according to the goals written on that team's card, then allow team members to make an attempt. Using the flip chart, record the team designation and its score. After all teams have completed their attempts, determine the winning team.

Variation

Suspend a rope approximately three feet off the ground. Have the members from each team form a circle, face away from each other, then hold hands. Keeping this formation, each team will attempt to cross over the rope without touching it and without letting go.

Discussion

- How did you as an individual feel about participating in this activity?
- How well did members of your team work together?
- How did the inability to speak affect your team's efforts during the first attempt?
- What factors did your team consider when setting its goal for the second attempt?
- Overall, how well do your think your team performed? Why?

Give and Take

Objective

To persuade another individual to accept an opposing viewpoint.

Applications

- Communication
- Conflict Management
- Negotiation
- Perception

Group Size

Six to thirty participants, who will work in teams of three members each. A minimum of two teams is required.

Time Required

Fifteen to twenty minutes.

Materials

One sheet of paper and a pencil for each participant; clock or timer.

Preparation

None.

Process

1. Distribute a blank sheet of paper and a pencil to each participant. Explain that each person is to think of a prized possession, something that he or she has and likes very much, and to write it down on the paper.

2. Instruct the participants to form teams of three members each. Within each group, one member is to be designated *Lender*, another *Borrower*, and the third *Observer*.

3. Explain that the participants are to imagine that Lender has loaned Borrower his prize possession, and Borrower has kept it far too long. Lender is to try to talk Borrower into returning the possession, while Borrower is to try to talk Lender into letting it be kept for a longer period of time. Two minutes will be allowed for this negotiation. The Observer is to watch the interaction that takes place closely, using the other side of the paper to note the strategies used by both the Lender and the Borrower, as well as communication patterns, body language, and other signs.

4. Signal for the negotiations to begin, then call time after two minutes.

5. Tell the Observers that they will have one minute to comment on their observations to the Lender and Borrower. Signal to begin, then stop the discussion after one minute.

6. Direct the teams to change roles so that the Observer becomes the Lender, the Lender becomes the Borrower, and the Borrower acts as Observer. Play a second round according to the previous instructions, then repeat for a third round so that each participant has the opportunity to play each role.

Discussion

- What were some of the observations made in the course of the negotiations?
- How do our personal expectations and feelings impact the communication process?
- How does this apply to managing and resolving conflict situations?
- What strategies did Lenders use to convince the Borrowers of their views?
- What could Lenders have done differently to be more effective in persuading the Borrowers of their needs?

Goal Tending

Objective

To establish a positive climate and spirit of cooperation in setting team goals for future development.

Applications

- Change
- Decision Making
- Goal Setting
- Team Dynamics

Group Size

Four to thirty participants, who will work in teams of four to six members each. *Note:* This activity is most effective when used with intact work teams.

Time Required

Forty-five to sixty minutes.

Materials

One sheet of paper and a pencil for each team; clock or timer.

Preparation

None.

Process

1. Instruct the participants to form teams of four to six members each.

2. Explain that each team will be developing a collective mental image (verbalized) of what its work situation should preferably be like a year from now. Announce that teams will have ten minutes for discussion.

3. Signal for the discussion to begin. Time the discussion for ten minutes, giving a two-minute warning; then stop the activity.

4. Distribute a sheet of paper and a pencil to each team.

5. Explain that each group is to develop a skeletal action plan, listing the items directly or indirectly *under their control* that must be accomplished in the next year to achieve the overall image the group members have described. Announce that teams will have twenty minutes for this part of the task.

5. Signal for the discussion to begin. Time the activity for twenty minutes, giving a five-minute warning; then call time.

6. Direct each team, in turn, to present a brief report to the total group.

Discussion

- How feasible is your overall plan? Is it possible to achieve your desired objectives a year from now?

- What factors may prevent you from being successful? (Lack of resources, unforeseen events, lack of agreement on goal or plan.)

- How will your team be able to keep its goals flexible in order to adapt to changing conditions?

- How often will you review your progress toward the goal?

Guest List

Objective

To examine group membership based on diverse roles and competencies.

Applications

- Conflict Management
- Decision Making
- Diversity
- Team Dynamics

Group Size

Eight to forty participants, who will work together in teams of four members each. A minimum of two teams is required.

Time Required

Thirty minutes.

Materials

One copy of the Individual Guest List Handout and a pencil for each participant; one copy of the Team Guest List Handout for each team; clock or timer.

Preparation

None.

Process

1. Instruct participants to form teams of four members each.

2. Explain that each member of the group is going away to a remote island for the rest of his or her life. The island has all the necessary items (food, shelter, water) needed for survival. However, the island is totally unpopulated. Each person is to choose any three people, currently living, to take to the island. The people must have the skills, backgrounds, and experiences necessary to live together on the island.

3. Distribute a pencil and one copy of the Individual Guest List Handout to each participant. Instruct participants to work alone, listing the three people they would like to take and why. Announce that they will have approximately five minutes for individual work.

4. When everyone has completed this portion of the activity, instruct each group to discuss the lists its individual members have completed. Announce that teams should spend no more than five minutes for this discussion.

5. After five minutes, stop the group discussion. Explain that the transport plane can only carry ten people: the pilot, the four members of the team, and five guests. Therefore, each group will have fifteen minutes to compile a listing of the five people they will take with them and why. Give each team a copy of the Team Guest List Handout and emphasize that all members of the group must agree on the final listing.

6. Signal for the activity to begin. Time the discussion for fifteen minutes, giving a five-minute warning; then stop the activity when time expires. Direct each small group, in turn, to present its list to the large group.

Discussion

- What are some of the characteristics of the guests listed by individuals?
- How did the lists compare across groups?
- How did your group decide who would be included on the final list of guests?
- Why were these people chosen?

Individual Guest List
Handout

Directions: List the three people you would like to take to the island with you and the applicable skills, backgrounds, and experiences of each.

	Who?	**Why?**
Guest #1		
Guest #2		
Guest #3		

Team Guest List Handout

Directions: List the five people your team has agreed to take to the island.
Include their applicable skills, backgrounds, and experiences.

	Who?	Why?
Guest #1		
Guest #2		
Guest #3		
Guest #4		
Guest #5		

Hike to Hideaway Lake

Objective

To arrive at a collective decision about provisions needed on a hike.

Applications

- Conflict Management
- Decision Making
- Leadership
- Planning
- Problem Solving
- Team Dynamics

Group Size

An unlimited number of participants, who will work in teams of five to seven members each.

Time Required

Forty-five to sixty minutes.

Materials

One copy of the Hike to Hideaway Lake Worksheet and a pencil for each participant; one copy of the Hike to Hideaway Lake Discussion Sheet for each team; clock or timer.

Preparation

None.

Process

1. Instruct the participants to form teams of five to seven members each. Each team is to select one person to assume the role of leader.

2. Distribute one copy of the Hike to Hideaway Lake Worksheet and a pencil to each participant.

3. Referring to the worksheet, read aloud the Situation and the Directions. Emphasize that there will be two steps in the planning process and that participants should wait for the signal before beginning or ending each step.

4. Signal for individual planning to begin (Step 1), then call time after five minutes.

5. Signal for team planning to begin (Step 2), and time the discussion for twenty minutes. Give a five-minute and a two-minute warning, then stop the activity when time expires.

6. Distribute one copy of the Hike to Hideaway Lake Discussion Sheet to each team leader. Announce that the leader is to conduct a group discussion based on the information provided on the sheet. Discussion time will be ten minutes.

7. Signal for the group discussion to begin. Time the discussion for ten minutes, giving a two-minute warning. Stop the discussion when time expires.

Discussion

• Based on the follow-up questions, how well did your team prepare for the hike?

• What are some examples of other unexpected situations that the hikers would have been prepared for, based on your team's provisions?

• How easily did your team reach its decision on what items to take? Why?

• What role did the leader play in the decision-making process?

• How did other teams' lists of provisions compare with yours?

• How do unexpected events affect a team's ability to plan or problem solve?

• If disagreements occurred during the team planning discussion, how were these handled?

Hike to Hideaway Lake Worksheet

Situation: Four friends are planning to take a hike to Hideaway Lake. They will be able to drive to within two miles of the lake, but because the road ends there, they will have to hike the rest of the distance to the lake. Each will carry an average size backpack. You must decide what the four hikers should take in their backpacks. You will discuss this as a group and make a list of exactly what will go into each of the four packs. Remember, they will be hiking over steep mountains, dry sandy gullies, and a wooded area to eventually reach the lake. They will be spending the entire day at the lake before returning. The area they are going to will be safe for swimming, exploring, and making a fire.

Directions: Think very carefully about the things the four hikers will need. If they forget to take something in their packs, they will be stuck the whole day without it. Also keep in mind the limitations imposed by the size of each backpack. At the end of the session, you will be asked some questions to determine how good your choices were.

Step 1: You will have five minutes to make a personal list of ideas on what items to include.

Step 2: Your team will have an additional twenty minutes to come to consensus on what items to put into each pack. The team leader will facilitate the discussion.

Pack 1	Pack 2	Pack 3	Pack 4

Hike to Hideaway Lake Discussion Sheet

Listed below are some things that happened to the four hikers. Did the various packs contain provisions to help them in these situations? Discuss your answers with the group.

1. One of the hikers cut his leg and it bled a lot. What items were packed that would have helped?

2. It was dark before the hikers decided to return. How did they find their way back in the dark?

3. They were caught in a rainstorm. What was available to help them stay dry?

4. It suddenly became very cold. What was packed to keep them warm?

5. They went for a short hike and got lost. How did they find their way back?

6. Considering the contents of the backpacks decided on by the team, what other kinds of unexpected situations might the hikers have been prepared for?

Jigsaw

Objective

To put together five puzzles from four sets of puzzle pieces.

Applications

- Conflict Management
- Negotiation
- Problem Solving
- Resource Use
- Team Dynamics

Group Size

Eight to twenty-four participants, who will work in four teams of equal size.

Time Required

Fifteen to twenty minutes.

Materials

Five simple jigsaw puzzles (ten to twenty pieces each); four medium-sized boxes.

Preparation

Combine all the puzzle pieces, then randomly divide them into four equal piles. Place each pile into a separate box.

Process

1. Instruct the participants to form four teams of equal size. Each team is to be located in a separate area of the room.

2. Distribute one box of puzzle pieces to each team.

3. Explain that the task is to *"Complete the puzzles."* Refrain from elaborating or answering any questions for clarification. In order to complete this task, members from the various teams are to meet in the "reception area" (a space designated in the middle of the room) to exchange puzzle pieces. During the exchange, teams are not limited as to the number of members in the reception area at any given time. However, these rules must be followed:

   - No player may carry more than one piece of a puzzle at a time.
   - Pieces may only be given. No player may ask, beg, entreat, or in any way request a piece of puzzle from a member of any other team.
   - When a piece is offered, it may be taken or rejected.
   - The activity ends when all the puzzles are completed.

4. Signal for the activity to begin. Call time when the five puzzles have been completed.

Discussion

- Who felt that he or she was in competition to be the first to complete the task? Why?
- Was there a winner and/or a loser? Explain.
- How were negotiations to exchange puzzle pieces approached?
- What strategies were developed for completing the task?
- How did the group as a whole handle the extra puzzle pieces?
- How well did members of each team work with those of other teams?
- How can we apply the *combined* concepts of cooperation and competition to the workplace?

Mancala

Objective

To remove all the counters from a team's side of a playing board.

Applications

- Decision Making
- Negotiation
- Planning
- Problem Solving
- Team Dynamics

Group Size

Six to twenty participants, who will work in teams of two or three members each. A minimum of two teams is required.

Time Required

Thirty minutes.

Materials

One copy of the Mancala Instruction Sheet, fourteen small container-like holders (for example, cupcake holders or jar tops), thirty-six small counters, such as pennies or beans, for each set of two teams; clock or timer.

Preparation

None.

Process

1. Instruct the participants to form teams of two or three members each. Have two teams form a "set," seated across from each other at a table. Designate one team as "A" and the other as "B."

2. Distribute one copy of the Mancala Instruction Sheet, fourteen holders, and thirty-six counters to each set of two teams. Direct the participants to set up the playing "board" by arranging the holders as indicated on the sheet. Next, they are to place three counters into each of the twelve holders, leaving the end ones empty. Explain that each team "owns" one side of the board, with the end holders being common property and belonging to both teams.

3. Explain that the teams will be playing a simplified version of Mancala, which originated in ancient Egypt and is one of the oldest games in the world. The rules of the game are indicated on the Mancala Instruction Sheet. The object is to be the first team to get rid of all the counters on its side of the board. Each play consists of the team scooping out all of the counters from one of the holders on its side of the board, then distributing these counters, one at a time, into each of the next holders, moving toward the right, including the ones on the end. If the last counter of the play lands in an end holder, the team has another turn. Review the example given on the instruction sheet. Announce that Team A will begin the game, with teams in each set alternating turns. Play is to continue until time is called.

4. Signal for the game to begin. Time the activity, allowing approximately twenty minutes for play to continue; then stop the teams when time expires.

5. Determine which team in each set won the game(s).

Discussion

- How did your team strategize its moves?
- How did the opposing team's countermoves impact your team's decisions?
- Did your team attempt to negotiate plays with the opposing team? Why?
- Could the end holders have been utilized to produce a cooperative effort with the opposing team? How?
- Why is a blend of cooperation and competition important in a global marketplace?

Mancala Instruction Sheet

Instructions: Using the fourteen holders, set up your "board" in this configuration:

Three counters go into each of these six holders

Team B side

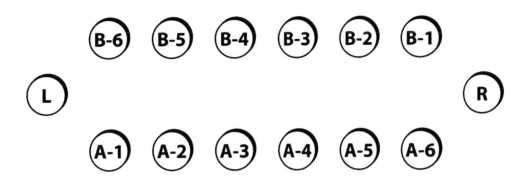

Three counters go into each of these six holders

Team A side

Rules:

• End holders (L and R) are common property and belong to both teams.

• A team's play occurs by scooping out all the counters from one holder on its side, then distributing these counters, one at a time, into each of the holders, moving toward the *right,* including the holder on the end.

• If the last counter of a play lands in the end holder, the team will have another turn.

• The first team to get rid of all the counters on its side of the board wins.

Example: If Team A chooses to scoop out the three counters from A-1, these counters would be distributed to the right, with one placed into each of holders A-2, A-3, and A-4 (each now contains four counters). The play is complete since the last counter was not placed into the end holder, R. The next play alternates to Team B.

Measuring Up

Objective

To estimate the number of items in containers.

Applications

- Decision Making
- Negotiation
- Perception
- Problem Solving

Group Size

Five to thirty participants, who will work in teams of three to five members each.

Time Required

Thirty minutes.

Materials

One each of the following items: jar, ball of yarn, telephone book, pincushion, pitcher, clear plastic box, bowl, bottle, pins, plastic bag, printed page; multiple quantities of the following items: macaroni noodles, cotton balls, mints, marbles, paper clips; water; one copy of the Measuring Up Worksheet and a pencil for each participant; one copy of the worksheet for the facilitator; ten index cards and a felt-tipped marker; clock or timer.

Preparation

Prepare the following items, carefully noting the exact quantity of each:

Macaroni noodles in a jar

Inches in a ball of yarn

Pages in a sealed telephone book

Pins stuck into a pincushion

Fluid ounces of water in a pitcher

Cotton balls in a clear plastic box

Mints in a bowl

Marbles in a bottle

Paper clips in a sealed plastic bag

Words on a printed page

Using the facilitator's copy of the worksheet, create an Answer Sheet by recording the correct quantity of each item. Using the index cards and marker, create one card for each item, writing a set of five *probable* answers (A through E) on each card, one of which is the correct answer. List the letter for the correct answer on the Answer Sheet. Display each item with its appropriate card.

Process

1. Distribute one copy of the Measuring Up Worksheet and a pencil to each participant.

2. Explain that displayed around the room are ten containers, each holding a carefully checked quantity of items. Participants will have five minutes to inspect them *without touching them* and estimate the quantity of items in each container. Referring to the card displayed with each item, participants are to enter the *letter* of the answer they consider to be correct on the worksheet in the column labeled Individual.

3. Signal for the activity to begin, then time it for five minutes while participants examine the containers, making sure that no one touches any of them during the process. When time expires, stop the activity.

4. Instruct the participants to form teams of three to five members each. Explain that team members are to discuss their guesses as to the correct quantity of each container's contents and come up with an answer on which all members agree. The corresponding letter for the guess is to be entered in the Team column for each item. Announce that teams will have ten minutes to complete the task.

5. Signal for the discussion to begin. Time the activity for ten minutes, giving a two-minute warning; then stop the group work when time expires.

6. Announce that you now will reveal the correct quantities and that each participant is to circle any correct answers in the appropriate column (Individual or Team).

Using the prepared Answer Sheet, indicate the letter of the correct quantity for each item.

Discussion

- How did groups arrive at a consensus for the estimates?
- On the average, were individual or team answers more accurate?
- What are some reasons for this?
- How does this activity relate to problem solving in the workplace?
- What role does individual perception play in problem solving and decision making?

Measuring Up Worksheet

Item	Individual	Team
Macaroni noodles in a jar		
Inches in a ball of yarn		
Pages in a sealed telephone book		
Pins stuck into a pincushion		
Fluid ounces of water in a pitcher		
Cotton balls in a clear plastic box		
Mints in a bowl		
Marbles in a bottle		
Paper clips in a sealed plastic bag		
Words on a printed page		

Mind-Set

Objective

To develop solutions to a series of problem situations.

Applications

- Communication
- Creativity
- Decision Making
- Diversity
- Problem Solving

Group Size

Eight to thirty participants, who will work in teams of four to six members each. A minimum of two teams is required.

Time Required

Forty-five to sixty minutes.

Materials

One copy of the two-page Mind-Set Worksheet and a pencil for each team; clock or timer.

Preparation

Duplicate, then staple together, both pages of the worksheet, one copy for each team.

Process

1. Instruct the participants to form teams of three to five members each.

2. Distribute one copy of the Mind-Set Worksheet and a pencil to each team.

3. Referring to the worksheet, explain that the teams are to discuss possible solutions for each of the five situations presented. They are to choose the most appropriate alternative and describe it in the space provided following the problem, along with the reasons why it would work. The answers are to be clear and concise in order to allow others to interpret them. Announce that teams will have twenty minutes to complete the task.

4. Signal for the discussion to begin. Time the activity for twenty minutes, giving a five-minute and a two-minute warning before times expires; then stop the discussion.

5. Direct the teams to exchange their worksheets so that every group has one other than its own. Explain that each team will be asked to read the response written on the worksheet it received.

6. Referring to the worksheet, read the first question out loud. Direct each team, in turn, to read the written response on its sheet. After all answers have been reviewed for this question, ask for a show of hands as to which alternative seems most feasible. Finally, reveal the answer given in the Best Solutions section below. Continue this process for the remaining questions.

Best Solutions:

(1) Because the dog is following every move you make, circle the tree several times. The chain will wrap around the tree until the dog no longer has access to the car doors.

(2) It does not matter where the fifth stick is placed, as the tree won't fall in any direction. Being wood, it will float and rise to the surface.

(3) Use a carton that is three inches shorter than the pole and place it in the carton diagonally.

(4) Use the dirt from the tunnel to build a mound high enough to reach the opening above.

(5) The statement was made on January 1 and her birthday is on December 31. Therefore, she was nine the day before yesterday (December 30), she was ten yesterday (December 31), and later this year she will be 11 on December 30. Next year she will be 12 on December 30.

Variation

Assign one question per team, with each receiving a different one. Allow ten minutes for teams to list all the possible alternatives and choose the best solution. Direct each team to read its question, then the proposed solution. Have other teams add any other alternatives not already mentioned.

Discussion

- How effectively did the team whose worksheet you received communicate its ideas?
- How does clear communication affect the way in which others implement our ideas?
- What decision-making approach did your team take for this activity?
- How does discussing a variety of different alternatives help a team determine a solution to a problem?
- What were some creative solutions to these problems that were not selected? Why were they rejected?

Mind-Set Worksheet

Directions: For each situation presented below, discuss possible solutions. Choose the most appropriate alternative and describe it in the space following the problem, along with the reasons why it would work. Be clear and concise in order to allow others to interpret your answer.

(1) You park your car under a tree and head toward a friend's house when a vicious dog, tied to a tree, lunges toward you. Luckily, you are just beyond the dog's reach. When you discover that no one is home, you turn to leave but realize you have a slight problem. The dog, straining at the end of his chain, is following your every move. Because the chain is attached to the tree, the dog has access to both doors of your car. How can you get into your car without the dog reaching you?

Mind-Set Worksheet (cont.)

(2) During construction of a dam, you encounter a tree 30 inches in diameter that is almost completely covered by water. In order to bring the tree down, five sticks of dynamite must be placed around the tree—one each on the north, south, east, and west sides of the tree and the fifth stick on the side to which the tree should fall. Because the current around the tree is flowing south at 2 knots per hour, on which side of the tree would you place the fifth stick of dynamite if you want the tree to fall north?

(3) You want to send your out-of-town friend a one-piece fishing pole for his birthday. Because you waited so long, you need to send it by air mail so that it reaches him on time. You find out that you cannot send the pole by air mail because it is three inches longer than post office regulations permit. You ponder the problem for a while, then realize you can still send the pole without exceeding the limit. How can you package and ship the fishing pole without bending or shortening it in any way?

4) You are out hiking and become trapped in a cave that measures approximately ten square feet. The surrounding walls are solid rock, extending at least six feet below the dirt floor. You realize that the only opening is in the rock high above you. You begin to dig a tunnel although you know that you will not be able to dig your way out. How do you plan to escape?

(5) The day before yesterday, your niece was nine years old. Next year she will be twelve. How is this possible?

Moonlight Serenade

Objective

To change a series of letters in occupational titles to form different occupational titles.

Applications

- Change
- Problem Solving
- Team Dynamics

Group Size

An unlimited number of participants, who will work in teams of three to five members each.

Time Required

Thirty minutes.

Materials

One copy of the Moonlight Serenade Worksheet and a pencil for each participant; clock or timer.

Preparation

None.

Process

1. Instruct participants to form teams of three to five members each.

2. Distribute one copy of the Moonlight Serenade Worksheet and a pencil to each participant.

3. Explain that many people these days work both a daytime job and a nighttime one. They may or may not be related occupations, but many times the job titles are similar. When that is the case, many of these people save money by using the nameplate sign from their day job and covering it with a sign segment to change it to the title for their night job. Referring to the top of the worksheet, give the example in which Bookkeeper can be changed to Bookbinder by placing the segment "bind" over the letters "keep." Give the following instructions:

   > Each of the occupational signs on the worksheet can be changed to represent another job by finding the correct sign fragment. The letters can cover the beginning, middle, or end of the original word. Each sign fragment always covers up the same number of letters it is replacing. Write the letter corresponding to the sign fragment next to each sign, as well as the resulting occupational title. You will have fifteen minutes to complete the task.

4. Signal for the activity to begin. Time the discussion for fifteen minutes, giving a five-minute warning; then stop the activity when time expires.

5. Review the answers through participant feedback before revealing the correct answers, which are given below:

   Answers:

   (1) B = REPORTER   (6) C = ACTRESS

   (2) E = ENGINEER   (7) J = BRICKLAYER

   (3) A = CARPENTER   (8) I = ARCHIVIST

   (4) F = DISPATCHER   (9) D = CARTOONIST

   (5) H = DEALER   (10) G = TRANSLATOR

Discussion

- How difficult was this task?
- How well did team members work together on this activity?
- What problem-solving approach did your team use?
- Was the approach effective? Why or why not?
- Replacing a few letters made a new word; how can minor changes have major impact in the workplace?

108

Moonlight Serenade Worksheet

Directions: Each of the occupational signs below can be changed to represent another job by finding the correct sign fragment from the list at the end of this worksheet. The letters can be placed at the beginning, middle, or end of the original word. Each sign fragment always covers up the same number of letters it is replacing. For example:

BOOKKEEPER → BOOKBINDER (BIND over KEEP)

Write the letter corresponding to the sign fragment next to each sign, as well as writing the new occupation.

1. | REWRITER | _____ |

2. | ENGRAVER | _____ |

3. | CARETAKER | _____ |

4. | DOGCATCHER | _____ |

5. | BUTLER | _____ |

6. | ACTUARY | _____ |

7. | BALLPLAYER | _____ |

8. | ARCHITECT | _____ |

9. | BASSOONIST | _____ |

10. | LEGISLATOR | _____ |

(A) PENT (B) POR (C) RESS (D) CART

(E) INE (F) ISP (G) TRAN (H) DEA

(I) VIS (J) RICK

Musical Islands

Objective

To promote a sense of cooperation in a competitive situation.

Applications

- Conflict Management
- Icebreaker
- Planning
- Team Dynamics

Group Size

Ten to fifty participants.

Time Required

Ten minutes.

Materials

Several cardboard sheets, sheets of newsprint paper, or small mats, equal to at least one-half the number of participants; radio or other source of music.*

---

*Note: If pre-recorded music is used, permission must be obtained from the copyright holder prior to its use.

Preparation

Place the mats, cardboard, or paper on the floor at various places around the room. Make sure that there is sufficient room between each to allow for ease of movement.

Process

1. Explain that the sheets represent "islands" and that the participants are to walk around the room while music plays. When it stops they are to rush to get on an island. An island may be occupied by several players, but any player who cannot squeeze onto an island or who falls off is eliminated.

2. Start the music and allow it to play for a short period of time. Stop the music and eliminate any player(s) not standing on an "island."

3. Remove one sheet from those arranged on the floor. Once again, play the music, then stop and eliminate anyone not standing on a sheet.

4. Continue with this procedure, reducing the sheets one at a time, until only one sheet remains on the floor.

5. The last players left on the final island are the winners.

Discussion

- How did you feel when you rushed to find a place to stand?
- How willing were players to help others find space on an island?
- How were conflicts resolved?
- What happened as resources (islands) became more scarce?

Nine Men's Morris

Objective

To place three counters in a row along a connected line.

Applications

- Change
- Conflict Management
- Decision Making
- Planning
- Problem Solving

Group Size

Six to sixty participants, who will work in teams of two or three members each. A minimum of two teams is required, and there must be an even number of teams.

Time Required

Fifteen to twenty minutes.

Materials

One copy of the Nine Men's Morris Game Card and eighteen counters (nine each of two different colors) for each set of two teams.

Preparation

None.

Process

1. Instruct the participants to form teams of two or three members each, then have teams form sets of two.

2. Distribute one copy of the Nine Men's Morris Game Card to each set of two teams. Provide each team in a set with nine counters in two different colors.

3. Explain that the teams will be playing a game called Nine Men's Morris. Explain that Morris games and their variations date back to ancient man, and evidence of their use has been found all over the world. A Nine Men's Morris board was found carved into the roof of an Egyptian temple dating from 1400 B.C. Shakespeare even alluded to the game in *A Midsummer Night's Dream*.

4. Referring to the top of the game card, read the rules out loud. Announce that team members may discuss each move before it is made, but that the opposing team may determine a limit to the amount of time allotted for discussion.

5. Signal for the game to begin, then stop the activity after all the sets of teams have completed play. Determine which teams won by a show of hands.

Discussion

- What was your team's initial strategy for playing the game?
- How effectively did your team adapt its playing strategy as the opposing team made its moves?
- Did any conflict arise among team members? Between opposing teams? Why or why not?
- What impact did these conflicts have? How were the conflicts resolved?
- How did your team approach the decision-making process?
- How did time pressures affect the quality of your decisions?
- How can we relate this game to various aspects of the workplace environment?

Nine Men's Morris Game Card

Directions: Teams alternate placing their counters on the board. If a team places three pieces in any row connected along a line, it can then remove one of its opponent's pieces. When all counters have been placed, each team takes one turn to slide any single counter to a vacant and adjacent point. Once again, three counters in a row along adjacent points entitles a team to remove an opponent's piece. A team wins when the opposing team has only two counters left *or* when an opponent is blocked so that no legal move can be made.

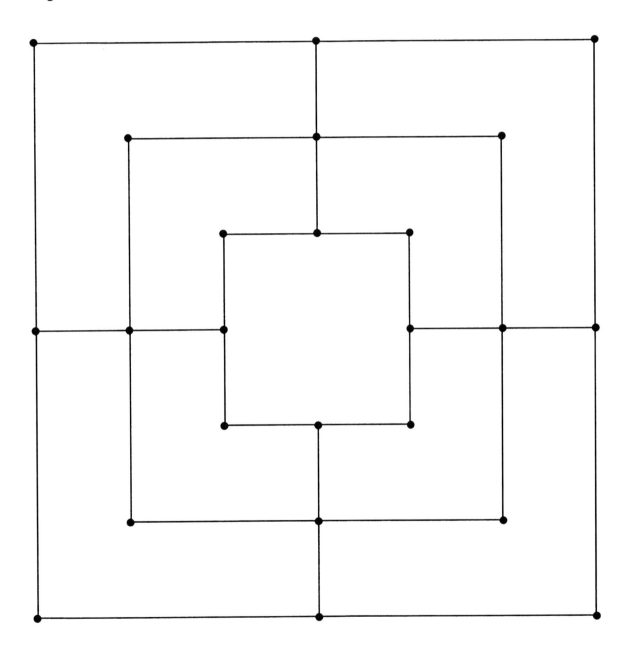

No Quibbling

Objective

To apply a set of rules for determining the correctness and translation of words.

Applications

- Change
- Conflict Management
- Leadership
- Problem Solving
- Team Dynamics

Group Size

Five to fifty participants, who will work in teams of four or five members each.

Time Required

Thirty minutes.

Materials

One copy of the No Quibbling Rules Sheet for each participant; one copy each of the No Quibbling Worksheet and the No Quibbling Solutions Sheet and a pencil for each team; clock or timer.

Preparation

None.

Process

1. Instruct the participants to form teams of four or five members each. Select one member of each team to act as the group's leader.

2. Distribute one copy of the No Quibbling Rules Sheet to each participant. Provide one copy of the No Quibbling Worksheet and a pencil to each team leader.

3. Explain that the teams have been hired to help prepare a new intergalactic newsletter. Their current task is to work on the article submitted by the inhabitants of the planet Quibble. This entails editing the spelling and translating appropriate words into English. The spelling rules for the Quibblean language are listed on the No Quibbling Rules Sheet. Review the rules sheet with the teams.

4. Referring to the No Quibbling Worksheet, read the directions out loud. Announce that the team leaders are responsible for assigning each member of the group a specific responsibility. Announce that teams will have fifteen minutes to complete the worksheet.

5. Signal for the discussion to begin. Time the activity for fifteen minutes, giving a five-minute and a two-minute warning; then stop the teams when time expires.

6. Distribute one copy of the No Quibbling Answer Sheet to each team leader. Direct the teams to check their answers against those provided. Allow several minutes for this to occur, then stop the activity.

Discussion

- How well did your team do on this task?
- What specific roles did leaders assign to team members? Why were these chosen? Were they effective?
- Did your team perform effectively overall? Why or why not?
- How did team members handle differences of opinion?
- On Quibble, would it be possible for a word to have two different English translations? Why or why not?
- Although the Quibblean words looked different from their English counterparts, the meanings remained the same. How does this relate to certain changes that occur in the workplace?

No Quibbling Rules Sheet

Spelling on the planet Quibble is phonetic, just as it generally is in English. However, as in English, there are some peculiarities in Quibblean spelling. These rules are summarized below:

1. There is no "m" or "n" on Quibble, but a single sound that is written as "mn."

2. The letters "z" and "t" always appear together. The "z" must follow the "t" at all times, except at the beginnings of words when the "t" always follows "z." The sound produced can be either letter or a combination of both.

   Examples: Ba*tz*mnamn, *Zt*ipkod, Ar*tz*mnkraf*tz*

3. An apostrophe always separates any letter followed by "q."

   Examples: Tramn'*q*wl, Rah'*q*mnrol

4. None of the above rules apply to words that begin with the letter "Q." Any word beginning with "Q" is correctly spelled no matter what, except that no word beginning with "Q" can have an "mn" in it.

5. All possible spellings are correct, except for the above restrictions.

No Quibbling Worksheet

Directions: For each Quibblean word listed in the first column, note whether it is spelled correctly (yes or no), the numbers of the spelling rule(s) applied, and the English translation.

Word	Correct?	Rule	Translation
1. Quiztqid			
2. Bahlb-Dmnr			
3. Tzumwareltz			
4. Emnstzrahqtz			
5. Quamn			
6. Nyahr'q			
7. Rabahdu'qui			
8. Quahgmnyr			
9. Wahtzub-daq			
10. Ztahtzahlfo'qtz			

No Quibbling Solution Sheet

Word	Correct?	Rule	Translation
1. Quiztqid	Yes	4	Quiz Kid
2. Bahlb-Dmnr	Yes	1	Bulb-Dimmer
3. Tzumwareltz	No	2	Somewhere Else
4. Emnstzrahqtz	No	3	Instructs
5. Quamn	No	4	Qualm
6. Nyahr'q	No	1	New York
7. Rabahdu'qui	Yes	3	Rubber Ducky
8. Quahgmnyr	No	4	Quagmire
9. Wahtzub-daq	No	3	What's Up, Doc?
10. Ztahtzahlfo'qtz	Yes	2, 3	That's all, folks!

Not on Your Life

Objective

To decide on life boat survivors based on individual persuasion.

Applications

- Communication
- Conflict Management
- Decision Making
- Diversity
- Negotiation
- Perception
- Team Dynamics

Group Size

Eight to sixty participants, who will work in teams of eight to ten members each.

Time Required

Sixty to ninety minutes.

Materials

Timer.

Preparation

None.

Process

1. Instruct participants to form teams of eight to ten members each and to sit in a formation resembling a life boat, with half of each group facing the other half.

2. Explain that participants are to imagine that they were on a cruise when a serious storm came up. Their ship was struck by lightning, and they have all had to climb into a life boat. The problem is that the boat only has enough room and food for a limited number of individuals. Two members of the team must be "sacrificed" in order to save the rest. The decision on who will leave the boat is to be made by group consensus. Each member is to try to convince the others that he or she should be saved. Announce that teams will have thirty minutes to make their decision on who must leave the boat and the reasons why.

3. Set a timer for thirty minutes and place it near the participants so that they can hear it tick. Give the groups a five-minute warning, then stop group discussion when the timer rings.

4. Have each group report its decision on who is to be sacrificed and why. Process the experience by using all of the questions below. Be sure to allow sufficient time for discussion, as this experience involves intense personal feelings and complex group dynamics.

Discussion

- Was this task difficult? In what way? Why?
- What kind of information did you provide to convince the group to let you remain in the boat?
- How did you feel about "making a pitch" for your own life?
- Did you learn anything about your individual values in regard to others' values? What did you learn?
- What kind of assumptions did you make? How does this relate to individual perceptions?
- How was the final decision made? How did you feel about the decision?

Observation Post

Objective

To list details pertaining to features of common items.

Applications

- Goal Setting
- Leadership
- Perception
- Problem Solving
- Team Dynamics

Group Size

Ten to fifty participants, who will work in teams of three to five members each.

Time Required

Thirty minutes.

Materials

One copy of the Observation Post Worksheet and a pencil for each participant; flip chart and felt-tipped marker; clock or timer.

Preparation

None.

Process

1. Instruct the participants to form teams of three to five members each. Provide each team with a separate designation, such as a number, letter, color, or shape.

2. Distribute one copy of the Observation Post Worksheet and a pencil to each participant. Explain that team members will have five minutes to work together to determine the answers to the questions listed. However, before the team actually attempts to answer the questions, direct each individual to write, in the upper right corner, the number of answers he or she *realistically* estimates that the team will be able to answer *correctly*. Allow a few minutes for participants to write their estimates.

3. Direct each team to select one member to act as leader. This individual will have final judgment as to the team answers and will record, then report, this information. Announce that teams will have ten minutes to come to a team decision on the answers.

4. Signal for the activity to begin. Time the group work for ten minutes, giving a two-minute warning; then stop the activity when time expires.

5. Review one question at a time by having each leader, in turn, report the team's answer. After all responses have been offered, reveal the correct answer using the Answers section below. Continue with this procedure until all questions have been reviewed.

   Answers:

(1) Franklin D. Roosevelt	(6) George Washington
(2) South Dakota	(7) right
(3) Thomas Jefferson	(8) middle
(4) Abraham Lincoln	(9) four
(5) Theodore Roosevelt	(10) U.S. Treasury

6. Instruct each team to count the number of its correct responses. Poll the groups to determine final scores, recording each one on a flip-chart sheet, along with the appropriate team designation.

Variation

Prepare a worksheet containing information pertinent to your organization to be used as a review after an orientation session.

Discussion

- How accurate were your team's answers?
- How close was your individual estimate to the actual number of correct team answers?
- What factors influence goal setting in the workplace?

- How does observation impact problem solving on the job?
- In what ways did working together as a team help your results? Hinder them?
- What role did the leader play? How does this relate to teamwork in general?
- How could your team have improved its score?

Observation Post Worksheet

Directions: How observant are you? Without consulting references, each team is to answer the following questions based on some commonly viewed items.

1. Whose face appears on a dime?

2. Which state borders Nebraska to the north?

3, 4, 5, 6. What four faces appear on Mount Rushmore (in alphabetical order)?

7. In which hand does the Statue of Liberty hold her torch?

8. On a traffic signal, in which position is amber (yellow) located?

9. When considering dice, which number appears directly opposite the three?

10. What building appears on the reverse side of a $10 bill?

On Fire

Objective

To identify words formed by connected letters within a jumbled puzzle.

Applications

- Goal Setting
- Problem Solving
- Team Dynamics

Group Size

Six to fifty participants, who will work in teams of three to five members each. A minimum of two teams is required.

Time Required

Fifteen minutes.

Materials

One copy of the On Fire Worksheet and a pencil for each participant; clock or timer; flip chart and felt-tipped marker.

Preparation

Prepare a flip chart with the following list of words, keeping the sheet concealed:

(1) Alarm	(5) Escape	(9) Power
(2) Ant	(6) Fighter	(10) Sale
(3) Arm	(7) Fly	(11) Wood
(4) Cracker	(8) Place	(12) Works

Process

1. Instruct the participants to form teams of three to five members each.
2. Distribute one copy of the On Fire Worksheet and a pencil to each participant.
3. Referring to the worksheet, read the directions at the top of the page. Direct participants to write down the number of words they feel their team will be able to locate within the ten-minute time allotment.
4. Signal for the teams to begin. Time the activity for ten minutes, giving a two-minute warning; then stop the activity when time expires.
5. Reveal the list of words on the prepared flip-chart sheet and direct team members to count the number of correct responses. Determine the team with the highest number.

Discussion

- How did individual estimates within your team compare with its actual performance?
- Were the individual estimates within your team very similar or very different? Why was this?
- What strategy did your team use to accomplish this task?
- Were there distinct roles for each member of your team? Why or why not?
- How does this activity relate to team problem solving? Goal setting?

On Fire Worksheet

Directions: Within the puzzle square below, there are twelve words that relate to the word *"fire."* To find the words, start with any letter and move horizontally, vertically, or diagonally to a neighboring letter. A letter cannot be used twice consecutively, but it can be used more than once in a word. Each word is three letters or more. The first word, alphabetically, has been given to you to help you start.

Before your team begins its task, estimate how many of the additional eleven words *you* think the team will be able to locate in the ten minutes allotted.

Wait for the signal before your team begins.

O	D	W	M	T
P	O	R	E	H
E	A	C	K	G
L	S	N	S	I
P	T	Y	L	F

1. *Alarm*

2. _____

3. _____

4. _____

5. _____

6. _____

7. _____

8. _____

9. _____

10. _____

11. _____

12. _____

Outer Limits

Objective

To determine individual levels of social discomfort.

Applications

- Diversity
- Perception
- Team Dynamics

Group Size

Six to forty participants, who will work in teams of six to ten members each.

Time Required

Twenty to thirty minutes.

Materials

One copy of the Outer Limits Worksheet and a pencil for each participant; one copy of the Outer Limits Tally Sheet for each team; clock or timer.

Preparation

None.

Process

1. Distribute one copy of the Outer Limits Worksheet and a pencil to each participant.

2. Referring to the worksheet, explain that each participant is to assume that he or she has been asked to do each of the listed activities alone, with the entire group as an audience. Tell them to number each activity according to the degree of discomfort it would cause them, with "1" being the most *comfortable* and "10" being the most *uncomfortable.*

3. After everyone has completed the worksheet, instruct the participants to form teams of six to ten members each.

4. Distribute one copy of the Outer Limits Tally Sheet to each team. Announce that each team is to compile an average ranking for the listed items by adding all the rankings together for each one, then dividing by the number of team members in the group. Tell them to compare their team rankings with the individual rankings and to discuss reasons why individuals ranked particular items. Announce that teams will have fifteen minutes to complete the activity.

5. Signal for the activity to begin. Time the discussion for fifteen minutes, giving a five-minute warning; then stop the activity when time expires.

6. Ask for volunteers to actually perform some activities of their choice. If there are no volunteers, proceed to the discussion questions.

Discussion

- How did team rankings compare to individual rankings?
- What are some of the beliefs that would cause a person to feel uncomfortable or embarrassed in front of others?
- What are the sources of these beliefs?
- What is the relationship between actually *doing* these activities and *thinking* about having to do them?
- Would you feel equally uncomfortable if you were in front of a group of complete strangers? Your family? Your friends? Why?

Outer Limits Worksheet

Directions: Assume you were asked to do each of the following activities alone in front of this entire group. Number each activity according to the degree of discomfort it would cause you, with "1" being the most *comfortable* and "10" being the most *uncomfortable.*

_____ A. Oink like a pig.

_____ B. Dance.

_____ C. Tell a five-minute story about your personal life.

_____ D. Sing a song.

_____ E. Hug the person next to you.

_____ F. Stand with your back to someone of the opposite sex and hold hands.

_____ G. Strut around the room like a rooster.

_____ H. Act out a scene from Shakespeare.

_____ I. Read a love letter you have written to someone.

_____ J. Throw darts at a target.

Outer Limits Tally Sheet

Directions: To obtain the average team ranking for each item, (1) add all the individual ranks for your team and (2) divide this total by the number of team members in your group.

Item	Total of All Individual Ranks	Number of Members in Team	Average Team Rank
A			
B			
C			
D			
E			
F			
G			
H			
I			
J			

Parallel Proportions

Objective

To examine conceptual relationships in problem solving by completing analograms.

Applications

- Communication
- Creativity
- Perception
- Problem Solving
- Team Dynamics

Group Size

Unlimited participants, who will work in teams of three members each.

Time Required

Fifteen to twenty minutes.

Materials

One Parallel Proportions Worksheet and pencil for each participant; clock or timer.

Preparation

None.

Process

1. Instruct the participants to form teams of three members each.

2. Distribute one copy of the Parallel Proportions Worksheet and a pencil to each participant.

3. Explain that team members will work together to solve the worksheet, which contains twelve analograms. The first two items in each statement bear a relationship that is shared by a second pair of words. Give the following example:

> In the statement "DOG is to PUPPY as CAT is to KITTEN," dog and puppy share the same kind of relationship as cat and kitten; that is, the second word describes the young form of each animal listed.

4. Referring to the worksheet, explain that the words to be placed in the blanks to complete the second half of each analogy are arranged alphabetically at the bottom of the page. Emphasize that each word may be used only once. Announce that teams will have ten minutes to complete the exercise.

5. Signal for the discussion to begin. Time the activity for ten minutes, giving a two-minute warning; then stop group work when time expires.

6. Review each completed analogy, one at a time, by first obtaining group feedback, then revealing the word pairs for each statement as given below.

Answers:

(1) compass/needle	(9) bank/river
(2) china/crack	(10) eye/jay ("I/J")
(3) tear/tore	(11) bay/wolf
(4) lamp/sunshine	(12) tooth/saw
(5) lion/pride	(13) snow/television
(6) enlarge/general (anagram)	(14) roof/mouth
(7) alphabet/letter	(15) skate/ice
(8) start/finish	

Discussion

- What made some of these analograms more difficult to solve than others?
- What role did perception (personal view) play in approaching the activity?
- How do analogies help us look for answers to problems?
- How well did your team work together in accomplishing this task?
- What could have been done to make your team's efforts more effective?

Parallel Proportions Worksheet

Directions: Twelve analogies are listed below. The first two items in each statement bear a relationship that is shared by a second pair of words. The words that go in the blanks to complete the second half of each analogy are arranged alphabetically at the end of this worksheet. Each word can be used only once.

1. WATCH is to HAND as _____ is to _____

2. STOCKING is to RUN as _____ is to _____

3. SEE is to SAW as _____ is to _____

4. FAN is to BREEZE as _____ is to _____

5. COW is to HERD as _____ is to _____

6. ENGLISH is to SHINGLE as _____ is to _____

7. SCALE is to NOTE as _____ is to _____

8. PURCHASE is to SELL as _____ is to _____

9. CURB is to STREET as _____ is to _____

10. OWE is to PEA as _____ is to _____

11. CROW is to ROOSTER as _____ is to _____

12. PICKET is to FENCE as _____ is to _____

13. STATIC is to RADIO as _____ is to _____

14. CEILING is to ROOM as _____ is to _____

15. CAR is to ROAD as _____ is to _____

ALPHABET	BANK	BAY	CHINA	COMPASS
CRACK	ENLARGE	EYE	FINISH	GENERAL
ICE	JAY	LAMP	LETTER	LION
MOUTH	NEEDLE	PRIDE	RIVER	ROOF
SAW	SNOW	SKATE	START	SUNSHINE
TEAR	TELEVISION	TOOTH	TORE	WOLF

Perfect Square

Objective

To form a perfect square from rope without seeing or speaking.

Applications

- Communication
- Leadership
- Planning
- Team Dynamics

Group Size

Eight to forty participants, who will work in teams of eight to ten members each.

Time Required

Twenty to thirty minutes.

Materials

One fifteen-foot clothesline rope, one copy of the Perfect Square Observer Sheet and a pencil for each team; masking tape; blindfolds (optional); scissors; clock or timer.

Preparation

Cut a clothesline rope into fifteen-foot lengths. Cut as many pieces as you will have teams.

Process

1. Instruct the participants to form teams of eight to ten members each and to move to separate areas of the room. (Allow sufficient room for movement.) Designate one person from each team as the observer and one person as the leader.

2. Distribute one fifteen-foot length of rope, four small pieces of masking tape, one copy of the Perfect Square Observer Sheet, and a pencil to each team.

3. Explain that the goal of the activity is for each team to form a perfect square with the rope, taping the corners to the floor. This must be accomplished without vision and without verbal communication. Explain that, before beginning the task, each team will be given a five-minute planning period. However, during this time they cannot touch the rope. At the end of the planning period, teams will have another five minutes to complete their squares. When the task is completed, each team observer will be asked to report his or her observations of the group process during both the planning and construction phases.

4. Signal for the planning period to begin, then call time after five minutes.

5. Direct the participants, other than the observers, to close their eyes (or put on blindfolds) and to refrain from talking.

6. Signal for the construction phase to begin. Time the activity for five minutes, giving a two-minute warning; then stop the group work when time expires.

7. Have each team observer report, in turn, observations of both phases of the activity.

Variation

Have all the participants form one large team and form a single perfect square from a fifty-foot length of rope. Assign three to five observers, who will use the Perfect Square Observer Sheet to report on both the planning and the construction phases.

Discussion

- How did you feel during the activity? Why?
- In what ways do you agree or disagree with your team observer's comments? Explain why.
- How important was the role of the leader? Why did you need a leader?
- What strategies were devised during the planning phase?
- How well did team members work together in completing the task?
- What impact did restricting sight and verbal communication have on the construction phase?
- What could your team have done differently to have been more effective during the planning phase? During the construction phase?

Perfect Square Observer Sheet

Directions: Report your specific observations during each phase of the activity. Pay close attention to such things as planning strategies, decision-making processes, communication patterns, individual behavior, interactions among team members, and so forth.

Planning Phase

Construction Phase

Personal Preference

Objective

To identify individual likes and dislikes of team members.

Applications

- Decision Making
- Diversity
- Icebreaker
- Team Dynamics

Group Size

Six to twelve participants. Most effective when used with intact work teams whose members know one another fairly well.

Time Required

Fifteen minutes.

Materials

One copy of the Personal Preference Worksheet and a pencil for each participant; flip chart and felt-tipped marker.

Preparation

None.

Process

1. Distribute one copy of the Personal Preference Worksheet and a pencil to each participant.

2. Instruct the participants to each list five likes and five dislikes, then write their names on the worksheets. Explain that likes and dislikes can include such things as hats, short hair, TV programs, olives, blind dates, and so forth—anything except people's names.

3. After everyone has had an opportunity to complete the worksheet, collect them.

4. Explain that you will be reading the lists out loud and that members of the team are to try guessing which team member wrote each list. The individual whose list is being read should also guess that a different team member wrote it and not admit authorship. The team's consensus decision will be recorded.

5. Read each list out loud, using the flip chart to record the name of the person identified by consensus. Continue until all lists have been read. (Be sure to keep the lists in order so that you will be able to identify the correct individuals.)

6. After all lists have been read and answers have been recorded, identify the correct answers by referring back to the original lists.

Discussion

- Were any team members identified for more than one set? Why?
- How do individual preferences affect a team's ability to function effectively?
- Why is a diverse blend of personal views important to a team?
- How difficult was it to come to a team consensus about who wrote any list?

Personal Preference Worksheet

Likes	Dislikes

Personal Space

Objective

To determine which of one's possessions would provide a stranger with the most information about one.

Applications

- Decision Making
- Leadership
- Perception

Group Size

Six to thirty participants, who will work in teams of three members each. A minimum of two teams is required.

Time Required

Fifteen to thirty minutes.

Materials

One copy of the Personal Space Worksheet and a pencil for each team; clock or timer.

Preparation

None.

Process

1. Announce to the participants that they have been exiled to a space station, although the reason for this exile is not known. The location of the space station and its environment is also a mystery, as is any indication whether or not they may ever return. Each participant is allowed to take two other people along. (The other two people in the team.)

2. Instruct the participants to form teams of three members each. Direct each team to select one member to act as the leader.

3. Distribute one copy of the Personal Space Worksheet and a pencil to each team leader.

4. Explain that the orders state that each team will be sharing the space station with three other people. However, you do not know their identity, their origin, whether they speak the same language, or whether they will be hostile or friendly. Each team is allowed to take only four possessions with them, and the group will have ten minutes in which to decide what they are. Team members should thoroughly discuss the reasons for their choices.

5. Signal for the group discussion to begin. Time the activity for ten minutes, giving a two-minute warning; then stop the group discussion when time expires.

6. Direct each team to report on the possessions it chose to take and the reasons for each choice.

Discussion

- How might strangers who do not understand your culture, language, habits, and so forth react to the possessions you chose to take?

- How did your team's possessions compare to the ones chosen by other teams?

- If you were to meet members of other teams, how would you react to the possessions they chose?

- Did the team leader play a pivotal role in facilitating the team's decision? In what way?

Personal Space Worksheet

Directions: Your team of three has been exiled to a space station in an unknown environment for an undetermined time period. You will be sharing the space station with three other people. However, you do not know their identity, their origin, whether they speak the same language, or whether they will be hostile or friendly. List the four possessions your team will take and the reasons each has been chosen. Your team will have ten minutes in which to make its decisions.

	Possession	Reason
1.		
2.		
3.		
4.		

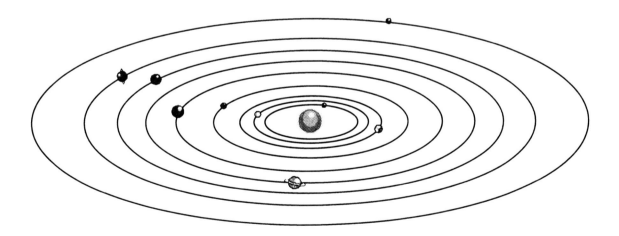

Pileup

Objective

To classify cards into the best arrangement to consolidate available resources.

Applications

- Decision Making
- Goal Setting
- Planning
- Problem Solving
- Resource Use

Group Size

Six to thirty participants, who will work together in teams of three or four members each. A minimum of two teams is required.

Time Required

Twenty-five to thirty minutes.

Materials

Twenty varied playing cards and one envelope for each team; flip chart and felt-tipped marker; clock or timer.

Preparation

For each participating team, randomly choose twenty playing cards and place them in an envelope.

Process

1. Instruct participants to form teams of three or four players each. Assign a different team color to each group.

2. Explain that the goal of this game is to reduce an arrangement of playing cards to as few piles as possible—ideally, to a single pile.

3. Describe the rules as follows:

   > A team decision is to be made for each move. You may pick up any card in the array and move it any distance *horizontally or vertically* (never diagonally) and place it on top of another card that matches it in either suit or rank. A pile of cards moves as a unit, with only the top card being relevant in determining where the pile may move.

4. Explain that the groups will have approximately fifteen minutes to complete the task. The team that reduces the arrangement of cards to the smallest number of piles will be the winner.

5. Direct each team to place its cards on the table in a grid pattern consisting of five columns and four rows.

6. Before you begin the activity, ask each team to predict the final number of piles it will be able to produce. Record this number on the flip chart next to the appropriate team color.

7. Signal for the activity to begin, then stop when all teams have finished or after fifteen minutes have elapsed.

8. Direct each team, in turn, to report the number of remaining card piles it has, recording each number next to the appropriate prediction on the flip chart. Announce the winner(s) as the team(s) that has the smallest number of remaining piles.

Variation

Rather than giving each team a random set of playing cards, give each team a duplicate twenty-card set. You can decide to have each group arrange the cards in the 5 x 4 pattern or you can supply all teams with the same pattern arrangement that you will display or distribute.

Discussion

- How close was your team to meeting the predicted goal?
- What factors affected the end result?
- Describe your team's decision-making approach to classifying the cards.

- What was your team's planning strategy? Did it change during the process? Why or why not?
- Because each card arrangement was different, how does availability of resources affect a team's ability to meet its goals? *Note:* This question is not applicable if you use the second option of the Variation above.

Playing the Links

Objective

To flip as many cards as possible by connecting ones that match.

Applications

- Change
- Decision Making
- Planning
- Problem Solving
- Team Dynamics

Group Size

Six to thirty participants, who will work in teams of two or three members each. A minimum of three teams is required.

Time Required

Thirty minutes.

Materials

One deck of forty-nine playing cards, three contrasting counters, one copy of the Playing the Links Tally Sheet and a pencil for each set of three teams; flip chart and felt-tipped marker.

Preparation

Randomly remove and place aside three cards from each deck of playing cards. Prepare a flip chart with the following information:

Rules of Play:

- Counter can be moved to any matching card in the same *row* or *column,* no matter how many cards are between.

- Same *suit* or *rank* creates a match.

- Flip card from which the counter was removed and score one point.

- No available move results in a forfeit. Game is over when no legal move is available.

- High score after two rounds wins.

Process

1. Instruct the participants to form teams of two or three members each. Have three teams form a set, with each set located at a separate table. Designate the teams as "A," "B," and "C," and select one participant as recorder in each set.

2. Distribute one deck of forty-nine playing cards to each set of teams and provide each team in the set with a contrasting token. Direct one participant from each set to shuffle the cards, then place them face up in a 7 x 7 grid. Each team is to randomly place its counter on one of the cards. Distribute the Playing the Links Tally Sheet and a pencil to the recorder in each set.

3. Explain that each of the teams within a set will play the same arrangement of cards. The teams will alternate, making their moves in sequential order, with team "A" going first. Referring to the prepared flip chart, review the Rules of Play that follow.

Rules of Play:

- Counter can be moved to any matching card in the same *row* or *column,* no matter how many cards are between.

- Same *suit* or *rank* creates a match.

- Flip card from which the counter was removed and score one point.

- No available move results in a forfeit. Game is over when no legal move is available.

- High score after two rounds wins.

4. Signal for play to begin, then stop the activity after each set of teams has played two rounds.

5. Determine the team with the winning score within each set.

Discussion

- How were decisions made within your team?
- How effective was your team's strategy?
- What impact did the moves of opposing teams have on your initial strategy?
- How well did your team react to the changes effected by the moves of opposing teams?
- How well did members of your team work with one another? With members of the other teams?

Playing the Links Tally Sheet

	Round 1	Round 2
Team A		
Team B		
Team C		
Totals		

Combined Scores

Team A	Team B	Team C

Quick Draw

Objective

To draw pictures and symbols that communicate perceptual concepts.

Applications

- Communication
- Creativity
- Diversity
- Perception
- Team Dynamics

Group Size

Eight to twenty participants, who will work in two equal-sized teams.

Time Required

Thirty to forty-five minutes.

Materials

One flip chart easel with pad and a felt-tipped marker for each team; Quick Draw Cards; Quick Draw Score Sheet; scissors; tape or push pins; clock or timer.

Preparation

Duplicate the Quick Draw Cards page on card stock, then cut it into separate pieces.

Process

1. Instruct the participants to form two equal-sized teams, located in separate areas of the room. Designate one team "A" and the other "B." Assign a number to each participant by having members from Team A count off, then having members from Team B do the same.

2. Place one flip-chart easel with pad and felt-tipped marker in front of each team.

3. Explain that one member from each team will be shown a card containing a word (noun) that describes a perceptual concept, for example, "anger." The participants then return to their appropriate team easel to draw a representation of the word for the team members to guess. The time limit for each round is three minutes, and the first team to guess correctly wins the point. If there is no correct guess, no point is scored for that round. The process will be repeated with new members from each team being shown additional words.

4. Begin the first round by randomly calling out a participant number. The member of each team with that number is to come to the center of the room, where they will be shown one of the Quick Draw Cards. Once the participants return to their easels, start timing the round. Stop the activity when one team makes a correct guess or after three minutes. Have the "artists" write the representative word on each drawing, remove them from the easels, then post them next to one another. Record the score for Round 1 on the Quick Draw Score Sheet.

5. Repeat Step 4 with new participants and a new word for Round 2. Continue this process for additional rounds, as time allows.

Discussion

- Was it difficult to communicate the representative words to others? Why or why not?

- Looking at the posted drawings, what were some of the similarities and differences between the individual drawings made for each word?

- How does an individual's interpretation of the meaning of a word influence its transmission to others?

- Why is it important for teams to have a common understanding of various concepts, such as trust and respect?

Honesty	Diversity
Respect	Fairness
Equality	Pride
Friendship	Courtesy
Trust	Loyalty

Quick Draw Score Sheet

Round	Team A	Team B
1		
2		
3		
4		
5		
6		
7		
8		
9		
10		

The Right Stuff

Objective

To duplicate a set of materials based on transmitted information.

Applications

- Change
- Communication
- Leadership
- Perception

Group Size

Five to thirty participants, who will work in teams of three to five members each.

Time Required

Twenty minutes.

Materials

One chart board for each team; one copy each of The Right Stuff View 1 and The Right Stuff View 2 sheets for each team, plus one of each for the facilitator; poster board, ruler, and felt-tipped marker; stopwatch or clock with second hand.

Preparation

Make one chart board for each team by marking a tic-tac-toe design on a sheet of poster board (approximately 10 inches by 12 inches).

Process

1. Instruct the participants to form teams of three to five members each. Direct each team to select one person to be the leader.

2. Distribute one chart board to each team.

3. Explain that the leader from each team will be given a brief opportunity to view a visual representation of a variety of items placed on a chart similar to the one distributed. The leaders will then return to their respective teams and describe the items to the rest of the members. Participants will have five minutes to locate duplicate items in their possession and position them appropriately on their boards.

4. Invite the team leaders to gather together in one location away from the view of the remaining team members. Reveal The Right Stuff View 1 sheet and allow them to study it for ten seconds. Tell them to return to their teams, where they will transmit information on the items they saw on the board.

5. Once the team leaders have returned to the groups, time the activity for five minutes. Stop the activity when time expires.

6. Distribute one copy of The Right Stuff View 1 sheet to each team. Tell them to compare the results from their boards with the sheets.

7. Repeat steps 4 through 6 above, using The Right Stuff View 2 sheet.

Discussion

- What were your reactions to the leader's role in your group?
- How did your reliance on the leader for transmission of information affect the task overall?
- In what ways does this relate to the leader's role in the workplace?
- Were the picture symbols or the words more open to interpretation? In what way?
- Which presentation was easier to remember? Why?
- How did the change from one form of presentation to another affect the process?
- How does this relate to changes in the workplace?

The Right Stuff View 1

Penny	Key	Ring
Stamp	Comb	Pen
File	Clip	Watch

Runway

Objective

To use oral directions that maneuver an individual through an obstacle course.

Applications

- Communication
- Leadership
- Problem Solving

Group Size

Ten to twenty participants.

Time Required

Fifteen to twenty minutes.

Materials

Objects that can be used as obstacles (boxes, cartons, plastic bottles, pillows, etc.); blindfold.

Preparation

None.

Process

1. Explain to the participants that the setting is an airport. Due to heavy fog conditions, pilots cannot see the runway and must depend on the control tower to guide them for the landing.

2. Ask for two volunteers, one to be the pilot and one to be the tower controller. Blindfold the "pilot" and have him or her stand at one end of the room while the "controller" stands at the other end. Have the remaining participants form a "runway" by standing down the length of the room in two lines that are approximately four feet apart. Tell people who are forming the runway that they are to remain silent during the activity.

3. After the blindfolded pilot is in position, place various obstacles on the "runway."

4. Explain that the tower controller must give verbal directions to guide the pilot down the runway so that the pilot does not touch any of the obstacles or go off the runway (touch one of the participants in line). Say that because the radio is not working properly, communication is one way only and the pilot cannot talk to the controller. Signal for the activity to begin, calling time when the pilot reaches the controller.

5. Select another pair of participants to act as pilot and tower controller. After the new pilot has been blindfolded, change the configuration of the obstacles.

6. Explain that this time the pilot can talk to the control tower (two-way communication). Remind the participants constituting the runway to remain silent. Signal for the activity to begin, calling time when the pilot reaches the controller.

Discussion

- What directions did pilots find most helpful? Least helpful?
- Which trial was more effective? Why?
- How did the pilot feel when he or she could *not* ask questions of the controller?
- How did the controllers feel about their responsibility for giving directions?
- What are the benefits of using a two-way communication process?

Scenic Route

Objective

To move through a picture maze by connecting word sequences.

Applications

- Communication
- Perception
- Problem Solving

Group Size

Unlimited participants, who will work in teams of two or three members each. A minimum of two teams is required.

Time Required

Fifteen to twenty minutes.

Materials

One copy of the Scenic Route Worksheet, one copy of the Scenic Route Answer Sheet, and a pencil for each team; clock or timer.

Preparation

None.

Process

1. Instruct the participants to form teams of two or three members each.

2. Distribute one copy of the Scenic Route Worksheet and a pencil to each team.

3. Referring to the worksheet, explain the following:

> Each of the pictures on the worksheet represents a six-letter word. The object is to move from the upper left corner to the lower right. You can only move to an adjacent picture (horizontally, vertically, or diagonally) if the first three or last three letters of the word that the picture represents are the same as those in the box from which you are moving. You may choose either half of the word to start, but the next move must be made by matching the letters on the other half.

> For example, if your first move were from WAL-*LET* to CHA-*LET,* the next can be to *CHA*-ISE, but not to GOB-*LET,* because that would be matching the last three letters twice in a row.

4. Announce that teams will have approximately ten minutes in which to complete this task.

5. Signal for the activity to begin. Time the activity for approximately ten minutes, then stop the teams when time expires.

6. Ask for participant input as you reveal the correct sequence.

   Solution:

   Picture number sequence:

   $$1 \rightarrow 5 \rightarrow 4 \rightarrow 8 \rightarrow 10 \rightarrow 13 \rightarrow 17 \rightarrow 18 \rightarrow 20 \rightarrow 21$$

7. Distribute one copy of the Scenic Route Answer Sheet to each team so that they can review the pictures and words and the solution sequence.

Discussion

- How difficult was this task? What made it difficult?
- What approach did your team take for solving this challenge?
- Were some of the pictures open to more than one interpretation? In what way?
- In what ways does personal perception impact how ideas or messages are conveyed to others?

Scenic Route Worksheet

Directions: The maze below consists of pictures that represent six-letter words. The object is to move from the upper left corner to the lower right. You can only move to an adjacent picture (horizontally, vertically, or diagonally) if the first three or last three letters of the word that the picture represents are the same as those in the box from which you are moving. You may choose either half of the word to start, but the next move must be made by matching the letters on the other half.

For example, if your first move were from WAL-*LET* to CHA-*LET*, the next can be to *CHA*-ISE, but not to GOB-*LET*, because that would be matching the last three letters twice in a row.

Scenic Route Answer Sheet

Solution sequence: 1 → 5 → 4 → 8 → 10 → 13 → 17 → 18 → 20 → 21

1	TAC<u>KLE</u>	2	CASTLE	3	CANDLE
4	*BUC<u>KET</u>*	5	*BUC<u>KLE</u>*	6	HANDLE
7	BASKET	8	*MAR<u>KET</u>*	9	MARACA
10	*MAR<u>KER</u>*	11	TURTLE	12	TICKET
13	*BAN<u>KER</u>*	14	TURKEY	15	WINDOW
16	MONKEY	17	*BAN<u>NER</u>*	18	*WIN<u>NER</u>*
19	DINNER	20	*WIN<u>TER</u>*	21	BAT<u>TER</u>

Secret Desires

Objective

To allocate a limited amount of money for competitive bidding on various items.

Applications

- Conflict Management
- Decision Making
- Diversity
- Negotiation
- Team Dynamics

Group Size

Eight to thirty participants, who will work in teams of four to six members each. A minimum of two teams is required.

Time Required

Twenty to thirty minutes.

Materials

One copy of the Secret Desires Worksheet and a pencil for each team; flip chart and felt-tipped marker; clock or timer.

Preparation

Prepare a flip-chart sheet with column headings for "Items" and for each team's designation. Under the "Items" column, list the letters A through J (corresponding to the items listed on the worksheet).

Process

1. Instruct participants to form teams of four to six members each. Provide each group with a separate team identification, such as a number, letter, color, or shape.

2. Distribute one copy of the Secret Desires Worksheet and a pencil to each team.

3. Referring to the worksheet, explain that the teams will each receive a bank balance of $100, which they may allocate in any way when they bid for the eight items listed. Say that each item must be bid on, and that the minimum bid is $1. All bids must be in terms of whole dollars only. Tell the teams that they will have fifteen minutes to discuss among themselves how much to bid for each item. Explain that they will then submit their worksheets with their final bids.

4. Signal for the discussion to begin. Time the session for fifteen minutes, giving a five-minute and a two-minute warning; then stop the discussion when time expires.

5. Collect the completed worksheets from the teams.

6. Using the prepared flip chart, post the amount that each team has bid for each item. Then circle the highest bid in each case.

Discussion

- Which team received the most items?

- Did your team have any particular method to its bidding?

- Why did your team bid the way it did?

- What item seemed to be most important, indicated by its receiving the highest bid? Why was this item selected?

- What factors influence individual values?

- How were differences of opinion handled during the decision-making process?

- Did team members try to negotiate to convince others to accept one item over another? Explain how this was done.

- Why is it important for leaders to understand the values of individual team members?

Secret Desires Worksheet

Directions: Your team has been given a bank balance of $100. You may allocate this money in any way to bid for eight items listed below. Each item must be bid on, and the minimum bid is $1. All bids must be in terms of whole dollars only.

Your team will have fifteen minutes in which to discuss and decide the amounts you will bid. Indicate your team identity on your worksheet, then record your final bids and give the sheet to the facilitator at the end of the discussion session.

Team Identificiation _____

	Item	Team Bid
A	Ability to make changes in organizational policy.	
B	Freedom on the job to come and go as one pleases.	
C	Lifelong good health.	
D	Happy and secure family life.	
E	$10,000 cash.	
F	National Outstanding Employee of the Year Award.	
G	Opportunity to travel throughout the world.	
H	Expertise at any one thing.	

Silent Moves

Objective

To invent a common language based on symbolic gestures.

Applications

- Communication
- Creativity
- Diversity
- Perception
- Team Dynamics

Group Size

Eight to thirty participants, who will work in teams of four or five members each. A minimum of two teams is required.

Time Required

Forty-five to sixty minutes.

Materials

One sheet of newsprint and a felt-tipped marker for each team; clock or timer.

Preparation

None.

Process

1. Instruct the participants to form teams of four or five members each.

2. Explain that each team represents a group of people marooned together on a remote island, none of whom can speak the same language. Say that each team must develop a common language in order to survive. It is essential that team members work together to gather food, build shelter, keep warm, and so on.

3. Announce that each team will have fifteen minutes in which to create its new silent language. Team members must use only actions to reach a common understanding about each gesture and the symbolic meaning it will have. Remind the teams that they are to remain *silent during this phase.*

4. Signal for the activity to begin. Time the groups for fifteen minutes, giving a two-minute warning; then stop the activity when time expires.

5. Distribute one sheet of newsprint and a felt-tipped marker to each team. Explain that the team will now make a chart that describes the gestures the members agreed to use and the meaning of each one. Announce that teams will have ten minutes to complete this task.

6. Signal for the teams to begin, then stop the activity after approximately ten minutes.

7. Direct each team, in turn, to post its chart, demonstrate the gestures created, and explain the meanings to the large group.

Discussion

- How difficult was it for your team to communicate without speaking?
- How well did team members work together? Give some examples.
- What similarities and differences were there among the silent languages each team developed?
- What concepts did each team feel needed to be developed into gestures for the group to survive?
- Were the gestures that were demonstrated easily understood by other teams? Why or why not?
- How does past experience influence the way in which we communicate with others?

Stringing Along

Objective

To construct the longest string of separate and varied yarn pieces.

Applications

- Diversity
- Goal Setting
- Icebreaker
- Planning
- Team Dynamics

Group Size

Ten to fifty participants, who will work in equal-size teams of five to ten members each. A minimum of two teams is required.

Time Required

Ten to fifteen minutes.

Materials

Several skeins of yarn in a variety of colors; scissors; clock or timer.

Preparation

Cut seventy-five to one hundred pieces of yarn of varying lengths—from two inches to several feet. Hide each piece of yarn somewhere in the room before participants arrive.

Process

1. Instruct all participants to stand in the middle of the room. Form a minimum of two equal teams with approximately five to ten members in each group.

2. Explain that you have hidden pieces of yarn in the room. The object is for each team to find and tie together as many pieces as possible. Explain that the yarn pieces are not the same length, and the winning team will be the one with the *longest* line, not necessarily the most segments.

3. Signal for the activity to begin, then stop at the end of approximately ten minutes or when it seems that most of the yarn has been found and tied.

4. Direct the teams to stretch their lines out side by side to compare length. The team with the longest string of yarn is the winner.

Discussion

- What kind of planning occurred within your team before you started the search for yarn?

- How well did members of your team work together to complete the task?

- How can you relate the pieced-together yarn strings to the concept of teamwork. [They are composed of individual pieces in a variety of colors and lengths, as teams rely on individual diversity of ideas, skills, backgrounds, and so forth.]

Symbolic Gestures

Objective

To express meanings by using both words and nonverbal symbols.

Applications

- Communication
- Creativity
- Icebreaker
- Perception

Group Size

Six to twenty participants.

Time Required

Ten to fifteen minutes.

Materials

None.

Preparation

None.

Process

1. Direct participants to sit or stand in a circle.

2. Explain that one person will start by saying a word, and then the person to the right is to respond to the word by quickly saying another word that he or she associates with the first one. Explain that play will continue until all participants have had a chance to respond.

   Give the following example:

   > The first person may say "glove," and the second person may respond by saying "hand." The next person in the circle will then respond to "hand" with another word, perhaps "finger," and so on around the circle.

3. Select a person to start the process and continue until the last person in the circle has responded.

4. Have the participants compare the word stated at the beginning with the last word given. Discuss the reasons for some of the associations made between specific words.

5. Explain that participants will play the game again, but this time will substitute nonverbal symbols for the words. For example, if the first person raises a clenched fist, the second person may respond by clenching both fists, the third may grimace, and so on. Select a person to start the process and continue until the last person in the circle has responded.

6. After everyone has responded, discuss what words might be used to describe some of the nonverbal symbols that were used.

Discussion

- How would you compare the way you feel in response to nonverbal symbols with the way you feel in response to words you hear?

- Were you able to respond more quickly to words or to nonverbal symbols? Why?

- Which did you feel more comfortable using, words or nonverbal symbols? Why?

Team Picture

Objective

To describe the ideal team environment by "painting a picture" with words.

Applications

- Communication
- Creativity
- Diversity
- Perception
- Team Dynamics

Group Size

Five to fifty participants, who will work in teams of three to five members each.

Time Required

Forty-five to sixty minutes.

Materials

One Team Picture Worksheet and a pencil for each participant (for the Variation, one worksheet and a pencil for each team); clock or timer.

Preparation

None.

Process

1. Distribute one copy of the Team Picture Worksheet and a pencil to each participant.

2. Explain that each participant is going to create a portrait of what he or she perceives to be the ideal team environment. Say that participants should first visualize the overall conditions and what is transpiring. Next, they are to use the worksheets to describe, in as much detail as possible, the conditions, the physical aspects of the setting, the demeanor of the team members, and anything else that gives a clear picture of the ideal team environment. Tell them to provide as much detail as possible. Announce that participants will have ten minutes to complete the assignment.

3. Signal for the activity to begin. Time participant work for ten minutes, then stop the activity when time expires.

4. Instruct the participants to form teams of three to five members each. Explain that teams are to discuss the descriptions that members have created, looking for commonalities and differences, then brainstorm ways in which practical aspects of these ideal scenarios could be incorporated into their own workplace. Announce that teams will have twenty minutes to complete the task, at which time each team will be asked to report to the total group.

5. Signal for the discussion to begin. Time the activity for twenty minutes, giving a five-minute warning; then stop the teams when time expires.

6. Direct each team in turn to report back on its discussion.

Variation

Form teams initially and distribute one copy of the Team Picture Worksheet to each group. Tell teams to develop composite pictures of an ideal team member and write a description in detailed terms. Each team would then report on its view of an ideal team member, followed by a large group discussion on the similarities and differences of the descriptions from team to team.

Discussion

- What were some common traits among the various conditions discussed?
- What were unusual characteristics of the conditions described?
- How can we account for the variety of views on the ideal team environment?
- How can individual perceptions impact the way in which a team operates?
- How could aspects of your ideal team environment be incorporated into the workplace?

Discussion for Variation

- What were some common traits among the various team descriptions? Unique traits?
- How can you account for diverse views of the ideal team member?
- What rules or guidelines could you incorporate within the team to help individuals meet the "ideal"?

Team Picture Worksheet

Time Capsule

Objective

To list objects and ideas representing the organization (or team) culture that could go into a time capsule.

Applications

- Communication
- Conflict Management
- Decision Making
- Perception

Group Size

Five to thirty participants, who will work in teams of five members each. Members of each team must be employed by the same organization.

Time Required

Forty-five to sixty minutes.

Materials

One copy of the Time Capsule Individual Worksheet and a pencil for each participant; one copy of the Time Capsule Team Worksheet for each team; clock or timer.

Preparation

None.

Process

1. Instruct the participants to form teams of five members each.

2. Explain that the participants in each group have been selected by their organization to prepare a time capsule that will be placed in a safe deposit box with instructions that it is not to be opened for one hundred years. Say that each team is to determine what should be placed in its own time capsule, and the items should represent the present culture of their organization.

3. Announce that each team will have approximately five minutes to select three items or ideas that it wishes to include in the time capsule. Remind them that all team members must agree on each item.

4. Signal for the discussion to begin, then call time after five minutes.

5. Distribute one copy of the Time Capsule Individual Worksheet and a pencil to each participant. Provide one copy of the Time Capsule Team Worksheet to each team for later use.

6. Explain that each individual on each team is to prepare a personal statement about each of the three items that would provide a stranger with an accurate picture of the organizational culture. Each statement is to be limited to twenty-five words or less, using the Time Capsule Individual Worksheet provided. Say that participants will have ten minutes to work on this task.

7. Signal for the team members to begin. Time the activity for ten minutes, giving a two-minute warning; then stop work after time expires.

8. Explain that each team will now discuss individual member statements and agree on which ones will be used to make up the team's consolidated twenty-five word statement that will be placed in the time capsule with each item. One member from each team should be selected to record the consolidated statement on the Time Capsule Team Worksheet provided earlier. Announce that teams will have twenty minutes to complete the task.

9. Signal for the discussion to begin. Time the activity, giving a five-minute warning; then stop the group work when time expires.

10. Have each team in turn report the contents of its time capsule by reading its list of items and the consolidated statements written on the team worksheet.

Discussion

- How difficult was it for the team to select the three items?

- Does the information in the time capsule accurately represent your personal view of your organization's (team's) culture? In what way? Why or why not?

- Were the individual descriptions easy or difficult to articulate?

- How did the team approach the task of integrating the individual descriptions into a team statement?

- Overall, did conflicts arise in the course of completing the task? How were these resolved?

Time Capsule Individual Worksheet

Directions: List the three items that your team has decided to place in the time capsule. In twenty-five words or less, describe each of these items in a way that would provide someone opening the capsule one hundred years from now with an accurate picture of your present organizational culture.

Item 1:

Item 2:

Item 3:

Time Capsule Team Worksheet

Directions: List the three items that your team has selected to place in its time capsule. In twenty-five words or less, agree *as a team* on a statement for each item that would provide someone opening the time capsule in one hundred years with an accurate picture of your present organizational culture.

Item 1:

Item 2:

Item 3:

Time for Teamwork

Objective

To develop improved teamwork strategies through the use of free association.

Applications

- Change
- Communication
- Perception
- Problem Solving
- Team Dynamics

Group Size

Five to thirty participants, who will work in teams of approximately five members each. (Most effective when used with intact work teams.)

Time Required

Forty-five to sixty minutes.

Materials

One copy of the Time for Teamwork Chart for each team; Time for Teamwork Number Cards; scissors; two small paper bags or boxes; flip chart and felt-tipped marker; clock or timer.

Preparation

Create two sets of Time for Teamwork Cards by duplicating the page on card stock, then cutting it into individual cards. Place each set of cards into a small paper bag or box.

Prepare three separate flip-chart sheets with the following headings:

General Associations

Applications to Teamwork

Relationships to Current Team Environment

Process

1. Instruct the participants to form teams of approximately five members each.

2. Distribute one copy of the Time for Teamwork Chart to each team.

3. Explain that the chart contains twelve different attributes. Say that each team will combine two of these attributes to make as many conceptual associations as possible. The words will be selected from the chart according to a pair of numbers that will be randomly assigned to each team.

4. Using the two paper bags containing the Time for Teamwork Number Cards, draw out one slip from the first bag, then one from the second bag. *Note:* If the second number is the same as the first, draw again. Assign this set of two numbers to one team. Repeat the process until each team has been assigned a set of two numbers. Direct the teams to locate two words from the Time for Teamwork Chart that correspond with the numbers received.

5. Place the following question on a sheet of flip-chart paper as the teams' first assignment:

   Using the two words assigned, what general associations can be made?

   Give the following example:

   Let's say that your group was assigned the numbers 10 and 12, which correspond with the words "conflict" and "communication." A *general association* can be made between these two words to show that "harsh words are often used when we have conflicts with others."

   Announce that teams will have ten minutes to complete the task.

6. Signal for the discussion to begin. Time the activity for ten minutes, giving a two-minute warning; then stop the teams when time has expired.

7. Referring to another flip-chart sheet, post the following question for teams to discuss:

   What general applications to teamwork can be made from the associations that your team created?

   Give the following as an example of how the previous association could be applied to their work as a team.

194

"Team members may feel lingering resentment if they use harsh words when disagreeing with one another."

Announce that teams will have ten minutes to complete the task.

8. Signal for the discussion to begin. Time the activity for ten minutes, giving a two-minute warning, then stop the teams when time expires.

9. Referring to another flip-chart sheet, list the following question that the teams will discuss:

> What are the relationships between your team's previous associations and the current team environment?

Give the following example:

> The previous association between "conflict" and "communication" can be related to current team environment by saying that "team members focus on being objective when there are disagreements and refrain from making harsh comments about other people."

Announce that teams will have ten minutes to complete the task.

10. Signal for the discussion to begin. Time the activity for ten minutes, giving a two-minute warning; then stop the teams when the time has expired.

11. Direct each team to report on its assigned words, the general associations made between the two words, how these relate to teamwork in general, and how they reflect the current team environment. Record relevant feedback on each topic using the appropriate flip-chart sheets.

Variation

Select one set of cards and assign the same attributes to all the teams or add a second set of number designations and have the teams discuss four attributes, separately and combined.

Discussion

- How difficult was this activity? What made it difficult?
- What new insights into teamwork were you able to acquire?
- How well do your work group members use appropriate teamwork skills in the current work environment?
- Which of the relationships discussed might be used to develop action plans to improve the effectiveness of your team?
- How can this particular technique be used to solve other problems on the job?

Time for Teamwork Chart

Time for Teamwork Number Cards

1	2	3
4	5	6
7	8	9
10	11	12
1	2	3
4	5	6
7	8	9
10	11	12

Tower of Power

Objective

To construct the tallest paper tower that will support a tennis ball.

Applications

- Creativity
- Leadership
- Planning
- Resource Use
- Team Dynamics

Group Size

Twelve to forty participants, who will work in teams of six to eight members each. A minimum of two teams is required.

Time Required

Forty-five to sixty minutes.

Materials

One copy each of the Tower of Power Instruction Sheet and the Tower of Power Observation Sheet for each team; fifteen sheets of paper, 12-inch length of masking tape, one pair of scissors, and a tennis ball for each team; one 2" x 3" index card and a pencil for each participant; tape measure or ruler; clock or timer.

Preparation
Cut a sufficient number of 4" x 6" index cards in half so that each participant will have one 2" x 3" card.

Process
1. Utilizing a large open space, instruct participants to form teams of six to eight members each. Provide each team with a separate number designation. Have each team select one person as leader and one as observer.

2. Distribute the sheets of paper, masking tape, scissors, and tennis ball to each group. Provide each team leader with a copy of the Tower of Power Instruction Sheet and a pencil. Provide each observer with a Tower of Power Observation Sheet and a pencil.

3. Referring to the instruction sheet, explain that each team is to design and build a tower that will support the tennis ball as high from the floor as possible. No props, such as walls, chairs, or tables, may be used. There will be two phases: Phase 1 will consist of ten minutes for planning, and Phase 2 will allow another ten minutes for construction of the tower. During the planning period, team members may use the material to experiment with structures, if they desire, but none of the material used during the planning period may go into the actual construction. In other words, no prefabrication will be allowed. Remind the observers to watch their teams' planning process and to make specific notes on the observation sheet provided.

4. Signal for the planning period to begin. Time the activity for ten minutes, giving a two-minute warning; then stop the teams.

5. Distribute one 2" x 3" card and a pencil to each participant. Direct each team member to reflect on how satisfied he or she was with the *process* that the team used in planning, as well as the *plan* that the team devised. Each person is to write the words "Process" and "Plan" on the card provided, then indicate a number from one to five to represent his or her degree of satisfaction, with "1" being very dissatisfied and "5" being very satisfied. Next, the team leader is to collect the cards and put them aside until the follow-up discussion.

6. Signal for the construction period to begin. Time the activity for ten minutes, giving a five-minute and a two-minute warning; then stop the teams. Determine the team with the highest structure.

7. Direct the teams to conduct a small group discussion for approximately fifteen minutes, with the observer reporting first. The focus should be on issues of collaboration and competition, leadership and participation, as well as procedures for making the process more effective and satisfactory for team members. Team members

are to use the numbers they assigned for their levels of satisfaction during the planning phase and relate them to the results of the construction phase.

8. Signal for the discussion to begin, then stop the activity after approximately fifteen minutes.

Variation

Substitute fifteen 4″ x 6″ index cards for the sheets of paper as the construction material.

Discussion

- How did the towers compare in their structural composition?
- How satisfied were members of your team with its performance in general?
- How did individual levels of satisfaction during the planning phase correspond with the results of the construction phase?
- Was there a correlation between views of how effective the process was and views of how effective the plan was? In what way?
- What were some of the positive behaviors exhibited that helped facilitate the team process?
- What were some of the negative behaviors exhibited that hindered the team process?
- How could your team have improved its procedures during the Planning Phase? During the Construction Phase?

Tower of Power Instruction Sheet

- Your team is to design and build a tower that will support a tennis ball as high from the floor as possible. No props, such as walls, chairs, or tables, may be used.

- There are two phases to the project. You will be allowed ten minutes for planning and another ten minutes for construction.

- During the planning period, you may use the material to experiment with structures, if you wish, but none of the material you use during the planning period may go into the actual construction. In other words, no prefabrication will be allowed.

- The facilitator will signal the beginning and end of each phase of the project.

Tower of Power Observer Sheet

Directions: You will be a *silent* observer throughout the process of planning and construction. Make note of specific examples of each content area in the chart below.

Planning Phase	Construction Phase
Positive Social Behaviors	
Negative Social Behaviors	
Communication	
Participation/Leadership	
Problem Solving/Decision Making	

Trade-Off

Objective

To negotiate trades of playing cards that complete a run by suit.

Applications

- Communication
- Conflict Management
- Negotiation
- Resource Use
- Team Dynamics

Group Size

Sixteen to thirty-six participants, who will work in four teams.

Time Required

Thirty minutes.

Materials

Two decks of standard playing cards; one envelope per participant; felt-tipped marker.

Preparation

Shuffle all the playing cards together. Using the list below, place the correct number of cards in each envelope, placing any additional cards to the side.

Participants	Cards
16–17	6
18–20	5
21–25	4
26–36	3

Mark the front of each envelope, consecutively, with the designation of either diamond (♦), heart (♥), club (♣), or spade (♠).

Create a flip-chart sheet with the following information:

Trades:

- Same number card, for different suit.

- Cards of one suit that add up to one number, in same or different suit.

Process

1. Distribute one prepared envelope of cards to each participant.

2. Direct players to look at the designation on the front of their envelopes. Indicate the four separate corners of the room as representing either diamonds, hearts, clubs, or spades. Have all the players with the same suit form teams in the appropriate corners.

3. Announce that the object of this game is to have each team obtain one complete set of cards, ace through king, in its own designated suit. When a team completes its card set, all team members are to return to the designated corner and raise their hands. The game will end when the first team to accomplish this is declared the winner.

4. To begin, tell each team to place the cards for its suit on a table or on the floor. Explain that duplicate cards from the suit, as well as cards from all other suits, can be used to trade. Members of the team should hold cards that are for trade and circulate around the room, asking for cards that their own team needs to complete a run in the designated suit. Referring to the prepared flip-chart sheet, explain that they may trade in the following manner:

   (1) A card can be traded for the same number card from a different suit, for example: three of hearts for a three of spades.

   (2) Several cards that are all one suit can be added up to trade for one card in the same suit or a different one, for example, ace, four, and eight of hearts (1 + 4 + 8 = 13) for a king of hearts or a king of clubs.

   Emphasize that an ace is worth one, a jack is worth eleven, a queen twelve, and a king thirteen.

5. Signal for the game to begin. When the winning team indicates completion of its card set, stop the activity.

Variation

To make the activity less competitive, in Step 4 point out that any duplicate card acquired in a trade must once again be traded away. This will prevent teams from taking out of circulation those cards that may be needed by other teams to complete their sets. For example, if both five's of diamonds were held by one team, another team trying to complete this set would be prevented from doing so.

Discussion

- How did teams plan for the use of their resources?
- How were trades with other teams negotiated?
- Were opposing players collaborative or competitive? How did this affect the overall task?
- What types of conflict behaviors, if any, were evident during the activity?
- In what way did time pressure (being the first team to finish) affect your team's approach?
- How does this game relate to activities in the workplace?

What's My Line?

Objective

To match cartoon pictures with their appropriate captions.

Applications

- Communication
- Conflict Management
- Decision Making
- Icebreaker
- Problem Solving

Group Size

Eight to thirty participants, who will work in teams of three to five members each.

Time Required

Thirty minutes.

Materials

One copy of the blank What's My Line? Worksheet for the facilitator; one copy of the prepared What's My Line? Worksheet and a pencil for each participant; one prepared Answer Sheet for the facilitator; ten to twelve cartoon pictures; one sheet of cardboard or construction paper for each cartoon; scissors and paste; tape or pushpins; clock or timer.

Preparation

Using magazines and newspapers, cut out ten to twelve cartoons with captions that contain similar themes. Enlarge the cartoons as much as possible. Cut off the captions, then paste each cartoon on a piece of cardboard or construction paper. Label each cartoon picture with a letter. Hang the cartoons on the walls, spreading them out as much as possible.

Using the facilitator's copy of the What's My Line? Worksheet, create a list of the captions from the cartoons, along with a few additional captions that have nothing to do with any of the drawings but for which the wording can be vaguely connected. Number each caption, ensuring that the sequence of numbers is not the same as the letters for the corresponding cartoons. Duplicate one copy of the worksheet for each participant. Use the original worksheet (or a copy) to create an Answer Sheet by listing the correct picture letter next to its appropriate caption.

Process

1. Explain that the object of the game is to connect the cartoon pictures displayed on the walls with their appropriate captions. Participants will first do this individually, then work in teams to come to consensus on the correct answers.

2. Distribute one copy of the What's My Line? Worksheet and a pencil to each participant.

3. Explain that the participants are to go around the room and try to connect each picture with its corresponding caption. They are to mark the letter of the picture on the appropriate line in the column marked "Individual" on their worksheets. Indicate that some of the captions are extra and will not be used. Announce that participants will have five minutes to complete the task.

4. Signal for the activity to begin. Time it for five minutes, then announce that participants are to stop.

5. Instruct the participants to form teams of three to five members each. Explain that the teams will discuss their individual answers and come to consensus on a set of corresponding team answers. The group answer is to be entered on the appropriate line in the column on the worksheet marked "Team." Encourage participants to reexamine the pictures if they wish. Announce that teams will have ten minutes to complete the task.

6. Signal for the activity to begin. Time the group work for ten minutes, giving a two-minute warning; then stop the activity when time expires.

7. Using the Answer Sheet, review the correct answers to the cartoon sets with the total group.

Variation

The game can be made a little harder and quite a bit more interesting if one key word is omitted from each caption and its position indicated by a dash. Each player must then not only find the appropriate caption but also supply the missing word.

Discussion

- Was this task difficult? Why or why not?
- What problem-solving approach did you take to arrive at the correct answers?
- Did you score better as an individual or as a team? Why do you think this was true?
- How were differences of opinions handled when the team worked toward a consensus?

What's My Line? Worksheet

Number	Caption	Individual	Team

What's Your Bag?

Objective

To illustrate individual identity through words and pictures.

Applications

- Communication
- Diversity
- Icebreaker
- Perception

Group Size

Five to twenty-five participants, who will work in teams of five or six members each.

Time Required

Twenty to thirty minutes.

Materials

One paper lunch bag and a magazine for each participant; two pairs of scissors and a roll of tape for each team; clock or timer.

Preparation

None.

Process

1. Instruct the participants to form teams of five to six members each.

2. Distribute a bag and a magazine to each participant; provide two pairs of scissors and a roll of tape to each team.

3. Explain that participants are to go through their magazines looking for pictures, words, or phrases that describe themselves in some way. They are to decorate the outside of the bag with representations of their "outer selves," then put inside the bag up to ten things that represent their "inner selves." Announce that they will have ten minutes to complete the task.

4. Signal for individual work to begin, then call time after ten minutes.

5. Direct the teams to have each member explain the representation of his or her items, first those on the outside of the bag depicting the outer self, then each item inside the bag to illustrate the individual's inner self.

Discussion

- How are self-esteem and personal expectations tied to perception of oneself?

- How does an individual's perception of himself or herself have an impact on the team as a whole?

- What are the ways in which we communicate our strengths and weaknesses to others?

- In what ways does a diverse work group influence team efforts?

- How closely related are your outer and inner selves?

- What factors influence how much we reveal of ourselves to others?

When It Counts

Objective

To work with an opposing team to complete a row of numbers on a game board.

Applications

- Change
- Conflict Management
- Negotiation
- Planning
- Problem Solving
- Resource Use
- Team Dynamics

Group Size

Six to thirty participants, who will work in teams of two or three members each. Each team will be paired with another to form a set.

Time Required

Twenty minutes.

Materials

Three copies of the When It Counts Game Board, two felt-tipped markers, and a pair of dice for each pair of teams; clock or timer.

Preparation

None.

Process

1. Instruct the participants to form teams of two or three members each. Then tell the teams to pair up with another team, with each one seated across from the other.

2. Distribute three copies of the When It Counts Game Board and a pair of dice to each set of paired teams. Provide each team with a felt-tipped marker.

3. Explain that the object of the game is for each set of paired teams to combine efforts to complete one row of six squares, *horizontally, vertically, or diagonally.* Teams will take turns throwing the dice, then make a mark on the square that corresponds to the number thrown, keeping in mind that the numbers shown on the dice can be *added, subtracted,* or used as separate figures in a number *combination.* (A double number is a "wild card.") Give the following example:

   A roll of 2 and 4 might be used as 6 *(added),* as 2 *(subtracted),* or as separate figures to provide 24 or 42 *(combination).* A double number (two 1's, two 2's) is a "wild card" and can be used to cover any number on the game board. Choose the number according to what is available on the game board. If no corresponding number is available on the card, your team's turn is forfeited.

4. Indicate that play will continue for ten minutes. Once a "win" has occurred for the first game (that is, a row of six squares has been completed horizontally, vertically, or diagonally), each pair of teams should continue to play additional rounds using the other two game boards until time is called.

5. Signal for the game to begin. Time the activity for ten minutes, then stop the teams when time expires.

Discussion

- How did you feel about collaborating with the other team to win this game, rather than competing against them?
- How effectively did members from each team work together to complete the task?
- How were conflicting ideas managed by each set of teams?
- What type of negotiation between teams was necessary to win the game?
- What steps did teams take, if any, to plan a strategy?
- In what ways did changing conditions play a part in this game?
- As you continued playing additional rounds, did your group's efforts improve? Why or why not?
- How does this activity relate to teamwork in general?

When It Counts Game Board

1	2	3	4	5	6
7	8	9	10	11	12
13	14	15	16	17	18
19	20	21	22	23	24
25	26	27	28	29	30
31	32	33	34	35	36

Wishful Thinking

Objective

To develop a list of strategies for improved teamwork.

Applications

- Decision Making
- Leadership
- Problem Solving
- Team Dynamics

Group Size

Six to fifty participants, who will work in teams of no more than ten members each. (Most effective when used with intact work teams.)

Time Required

Thirty minutes.

Materials

Three Wishful Thinking Slips and a pencil for each participant; one copy of the Wishful Thinking Worksheet and a paper bag for each team; scissors; clock or timer.

Preparation

Duplicate one sheet of Wishful Thinking Slips for every two participants, then cut each sheet into six separate slips.

Process

1. Instruct the participants to form teams of no more than ten participants each.

2. Distribute three Wishful Thinking Slips and a pencil to each participant.

3. Explain that each team will be visited by a special genie who can grant three wishes to help improve the team's ability to work together. In preparation for the genie's appearance, each participant is to write one wish on each of the three slips he or she has been provided. When completed, each slip is to be folded in half. Announce that participants will have five minutes to complete this task.

4. Signal for participants to begin. Time the activity for five minutes, then stop the activity when time expires.

5. Direct each team to select one person to act as leader for the remainder of the exercise. Distribute one copy of the Wishful Thinking Worksheet and a paper bag to each team leader. Instruct the participants to place all of the folded slips into the paper bags.

6. Explain that each team will have fifteen minutes in which to develop a list of three wishes that it would like to see come true in respect to improved teamwork. The team leader will read the collected wish slips and coordinate the decision-making process. Each team will be asked to present its wish list to the larger group.

7. Signal for the discussion to begin. Time the activity for fifteen minutes, giving a five-minute warning; then stop the discussion when time expires.

8. Direct each team in turn to give a presentation of its three wishes.

Discussion

- How difficult was it to come to consensus on the wishes for the final list?
- How well did the leader perform in coordinating the decision-making process?
- How can we make some of these wishes come true in the actual workplace?

Wishful Thinking Slips

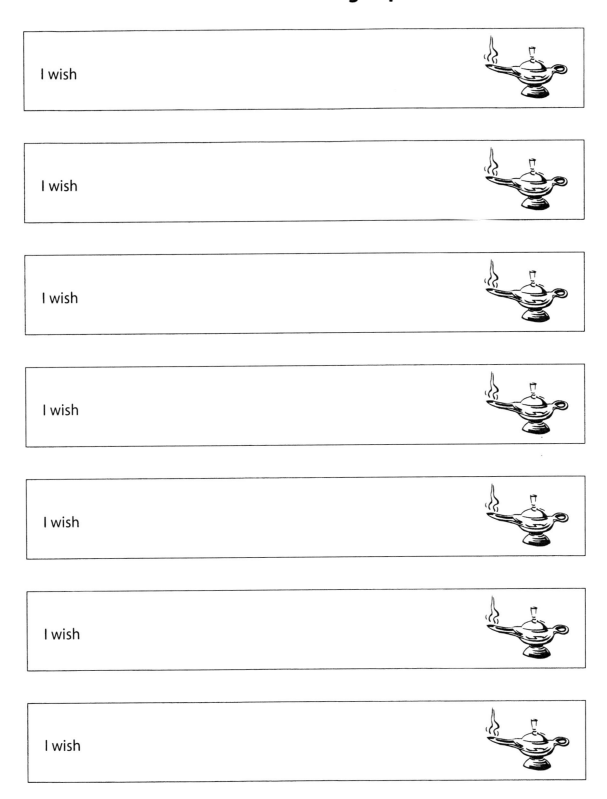

I wish

I wish

I wish

I wish

I wish

I wish

I wish

Wishful Thinking Worksheet

1

2

3

X-Acta

Objective

To develop a strategy for circling a line of X's that causes the other team to take the final one.

Applications

- Conflict Management
- Decision Making
- Planning
- Problem Solving

Group Size

Six to sixty participants, who will work in teams of three members each. A minimum of two teams is required, and there must be an even number of teams.

Time Required

Twenty minutes.

Materials

One copy each of the X-Acta Game Sheet and the X-Acta Worksheet for each pair of teams; one pencil for each team.

Preparation

None.

Process

1. Instruct the participants to form teams of three members each. Each team is to pair up with one other team, with one team being designated "A" and the other one "B."

2. Distribute one copy of the X-Acta Game Sheet to each pair of teams. Provide each team with one pencil.

3. Explain that this is a strategy game with two teams competing against each other. Each team will take a turn circling either one, two, or three of the X's, beginning with the one on the far left and working toward the right. The team that circles the final X will be the *loser*. The winning team will place its letter in the far-right margin.

4. Indicate that Team A is to begin Game 1; when that is completed, Team B will begin Game 2, and so forth, until all six games have been played.

5. After all the games have been completed, distribute one copy of the X-Acta Worksheet to each team. Referring to the worksheet, direct each pair of teams to work together to answer the strategy questions.

6. Allow enough time for all the teams to complete their worksheets, then review the correct responses by referring to the answers below.

Answers:

(1) First team.	(4) Circle one.
(2) Three.	(5) Opposing team.
(3) Circling one.	(6) Opposing team.

Discussion

- How did your team initially decide on how to approach the challenge?
- As each game progressed, did your team gain further knowledge regarding strategies?
- How did this impact your ability to become more effective in the games that followed?
- Were there differences of opinion among team members on how to proceed? How were these resolved?

X-Acta Game Sheet

Directions: Each team takes a turn circling either one, two, or three X's, beginning with the one on the far left and working toward the right. The team that circles the final X is the *loser.* Indicate the winning team for each game by writing its designation in the right margin. Repeat the game with the other team starting first. Continue switching the starting team for each game until six games have been completed.

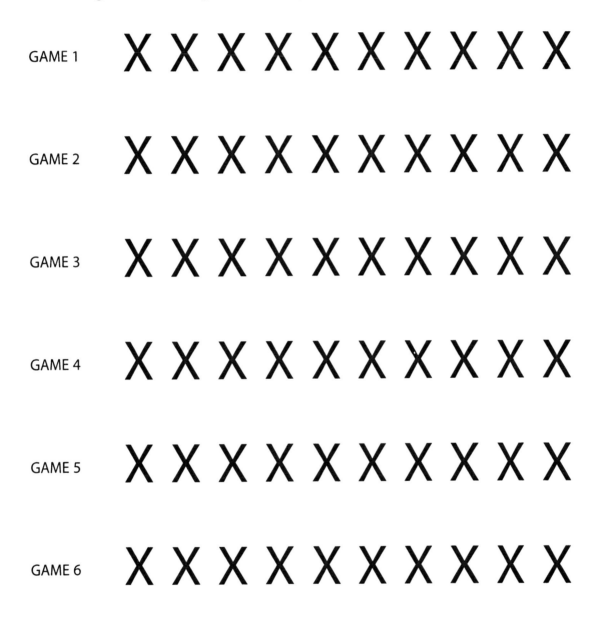

GAME 1

GAME 2

GAME 3

GAME 4

GAME 5

GAME 6

X-Acta Worksheet

Directions: After completing the six games, use the knowledge you have gained as a team to work together with the opposing team to answer the following strategy questions.

1. Who has the advantage, the team that goes first or second?

2. Which is the best first move—circling one, two, or three X's?

3. If the first team circles three X's, what is the other team's best countermove?

4. If the first team circles two X's and the second team also circles two, what should the first team do next to win?

5. If seven X's remain and both teams make the best moves possible, who will win—the team with the next turn or the opposing team?

6. If five X's remain and both teams make the best moves, who will win—the team with the next turn or the opposing team?

X-Change Rate

Objective

To acquire a completed card set by bartering with other teams.

Applications

- Change
- Communication
- Conflict Management
- Negotiation
- Team Dynamics

Group Size

Twelve to thirty participants, who will work in six approximately equal teams of two to five members each.

Time Required

Thirty minutes.

Materials

Six sheets of paper, each one a different color; six envelopes; flip chart and felt-tipped marker; scissors; clock or timer.

Preparation

Duplicate one copy of the X-Change Rate Card Sheet on each of six different colors of paper (for example, white, pink, yellow, green, blue, and goldenrod). Cut each sheet into individual cards. Shuffle the cards, then randomly place six cards into each envelope. Copy the following information onto a flip chart:

- 6 cards same color, 6 different designs
- 6 cards same design, 6 different colors
- 1 each of 6 different designs, 6 different colors

Process

1. Instruct the participants to form six approximately equal teams of two to five members each.

2. Distribute one prepared envelope of cards to each team.

3. Explain that the envelopes contains cards, each displaying a particular representation of the letter "X" in a specific color. Referring to the prepared flip chart, disclose that the object is for each team to acquire a complete set of cards, in any one of the following ways:

- Six cards of identical color, six different designs
- Six cards of identical design, six different colors
- One card each of six different designs in six different colors

4. Instruct team members to open the envelopes and examine their cards.

5. Explain that teams are going to barter with one another to try to complete one card set. Tell the teams that the first group to acquire a complete set in any of the designated ways will be the winner, but that the activity will last a maximum of ten minutes.

6. Signal for the activity to begin. Stop the activity when one team completes the task. If no team has accomplished this after ten minutes, call time.

Discussion

- How did you, as an individual, feel during this activity? Why?
- How willing were others to trade cards?
- What hindered the process?
- What methods did you use to conduct the bartering?
- How did the communication process influence the negotiations?
- How willing was your team to alter its original plan as certain cards became unavailable?
- How does this activity relate to the workplace?

X-Change Rate Card Sheet

Yurt Circle

Objective

To demonstrate the interdependence of team members.

Applications

- Conflict Management
- Negotiation
- Team Dynamics

Group Size

Unlimited participants, who will work in teams of six to ten members.

Time Required

Five to ten minutes.

Materials

None.

Preparation

None.

Process

1. Instruct participants to form teams of six to ten members each. Each team is to stand in a circle, holding hands.

2. Direct the participants to count off, alternating between one and two (that is, 1, 2, 1, 2, 1, and so on).

3. Explain that, at a signal, all of the number "1" people will lean *slowly* inward while the number "2" people will *slowly* lean outward to counterbalance them. Instruct participants to lean from the ankles rather than the hips so that they will not fall if not held tightly.

4. Give the signal to lean, then ask the participants to return to an upright position.

5. Repeat the procedure, reversing the roles so that the number "2" people lean *inward* and the number "1" people lean *outward.*

6. Explain that the Yurt Circle is named after the circular tent of the Mongolian nomads. The roof of the tent pushes against the walls so that the roof holds up the walls, while the walls hold up the roof.

Discussion

- How did this exercise relate to the concept of teamwork in general?
- How does the interdependence of group members impact a team's effectiveness?
- In what ways can we relate this exercise to the process of negotiation?
- In what ways can we relate this exercise to conflict-management strategies?

About the Author

Lorraine L. Ukens is the owner of Team-ing with Success, a consulting and training enterprise specializing in team building and leadership development. Her wide range of business experience, spanning more than twenty years, is applied in designing, facilitating, and evaluating programs in a variety of human resource development areas. Lorraine, an adjunct faculty member in the HRD graduate program at Towson University in Maryland, is the author of several training books and games, including *Getting Together: Icebreakers and Energizers* (Jossey-Bass/Pfeiffer, 1997) and *Working Together: 55 Team Games* (Jossey-Bass/Pfeiffer, 1997). She received her M.S. degree in human resource development from Towson University and is an active member of the American Society for Training and Development at both the national and local levels.

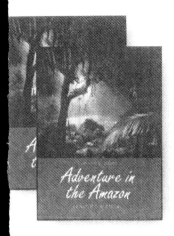

rraine L. Ukens

dventure in he Amazon

ctivity and Leader's Guide

this exciting activity, partici-
nts face a simulated "jungle
rvival." They must reach agree-
ent in this imaginary setting in
der to succeed, and they learn
y consensus produces the best
cisions.

When their plane makes an
ergency landing in the jungle,
rticipants need to decide
hich of 15 items on the
ane—including tallow candles,
pistol, safari hats, and other
jects—would be most essential
their survival. Participants
xperience synergy as never
efore!

e this gripping simulation to:

- *Improve* decision-making
  skills
- *Enhance* problem-solving
  abilities
- *Strengthen* group cooperation
  . . . and much more!

No one wants to write a team
ep talk" that could fall flat.
uman resource professionals,
am leaders, and managers will
ant to conduct this refreshing
ctivity with their groups and
eams in any work setting.

Activity / 16 pages • Leader's Guide /
16 pages
. . . .
Adventure in the Amazon Activity
Item #F451

Leader's Guide
Item #F450

Lost at Sea

Simulation and Leader's Manual

In this classic simulation, participants work individually then as a
group to assess fifteen items sal-
vaged from a yachting accident,
based on their value for survival.
Results are compared with the
expert rankings supplied by the
U.S. Merchant Marines. The
Leader's Manual offers instructions for facilitating the activity.

**In this simulation, a group is stranded on
a rubber life raft with minimal supplies
including:**

- Fishing kit
- Mosquito netting
- Shark repellant
- Shaving mirror
- Two chocolate bars
- And ten other items

Simulation / 7 pages • Leader's Manual /
10 pages
. . . .
Lost at Sea Simulation
Item #B630

Leader's Manual
Item #B494

Spark synergy in an icy wasteland!

Lorraine L. Ukens

Arctic Expedition

Activity and Leader's Guide

Activity participants embark on a
simulated journey through a
frozen, forbidding landscape, and
experience team synergy as they
never dreamed possible.

Any work setting is suitable
for conducting this activity. Your
facilitator, who does not need to
be a training professional, will
need a copy of the *Leader's Guide*,
which contains detailed instructions about running the simulation. Each participant needs a
copy of the *Activity*, the guidebook to this exhilarating experience.

In this icy wasteland, leaders
will spark a synergy that sets
teams afire!

Activity / 16 pages • Leader's Guide /
16 pages
. . . .
Arctic Expedition Activity
Item #F448

Leader's Guide
Item #F447

Includes FREE CD-ROM
with customizable resources!

Margaret Driscoll

Web-Based Training

Using Technology to Design Adult Learning Experiences

The practice of training on the Web and on intranets is growing at an explosive rate. People without technical knowledge need a basic guide that sheds light on best practices for web-based training delivery. People with technical knowledge need a savvy, practical primer on instructional design for web-based training. This is the web-based training book that all of you have waited for. Technical guides come and go.

> **"*Web-Based Training* is important not only because it demystifies web technology, but more importantly because it provides a critical link between the technology and the outcomes of learning."**
>
> —John F. O'Connor, educational technology integrator, Motorola University

What is cutting-edge today could be obsolete tomorrow. So *Web-Based Training* steps back from the technical whirlwind. This extensively researched handbook shows you how to create web-based training that adheres to the tried-and-true principles of great instructional design.

Learn how to:

- *Survey* the available training options
- *Prepare* organizations for web-based training delivery
- *Maximize* your training dollars . . . and much more!

This guide offers scores of case studies from both large and small organizations. You'll refer to *Web-Based Training* time and time again to pour over this guide's practical charts, tables, and checklists.

Self-study exercises reinforce readers' learning. Plus, the appendix offers a wealth of resources including a list of listservs and relevant organizations, along with a bibliography and glossary. The companion CD-ROM—included FREE with the book—contains even more resources: worksheets, document and presentation templates, job aids, and links to the Web.

"For those of us living and working with technology Web-Based Training is a refreshingly concise and easy-to-follow guide to ... successful implementation ... of technology-based training media."

—Tony Russell, UK education services manager, Informix Software Limited

"As an anxious technophobe, I found Web-Based Training very helpful and reassuring.... Anyone wanting to encourage adult learning through web-based training will find this an invaluable resource."

—Stephen Brookfield, distinguished professor, University of St. Thomas

Human resource development professionals have long needed a web-based training book that surveys the available options and makes reasoned recommendations for training delivery. The one-of-a-kind *Web-Based Training* forges the first path through this quickly shifting territory.

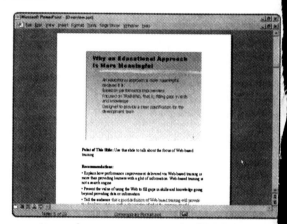

Among the many resources on the CD-ROM are PowerPoint presentations you'll use to explain web-based training to others!

SELECTED CONTENTS
- Before You Begin • Why Deliver Instruction on the Web?
- Principles of Adult Education • The Web-Based Training Process • Assessing Learner Needs • Selecting the Most Appropriate Web-Based Training Method • Designing Lessons
- Asynchronous Interactions • Synchronous Interactions
- Creating Blueprints • Evaluating Programs • Ready, Set, Go
- Glossary

---

hardcover / 256 pages / includes a CD-ROM
• • • • • • • • • • • • •
Web-Based Training
Item #F747

A career guide and a reference tool—in a single source!

Judith Hale

The Performance Consultant's Fieldbook

Tools and Techniques for Improving Organizations and People

Internal or external consultant, novice or expert, you've probably heard about performance consulting, a high-impact approach that blends old-fashioned facilitation skills with cutting-edge process and outcome analysis. You want to gain the expertise necessary to identify why an organization is out of alignment, what interventions will correct these problems, and how you can measure your consulting success.

This remarkable book is your skill-builder and resource guide. The step-by-step *Fieldbook* shows you how to make the professional transition to a performance consulting career. You'll use this guide to: • define and describe your consulting skills • determine the costs and measure the effectiveness of your consulting process . . . and much more!

Hale has done an outstanding job in this book of contributing to everyone's use of performance technology."
—Danny Langdon, president, Performance International

The *Fieldbook* details the techniques you need to conduct performance interventions and offers a customizable collection of worksheets, flowcharts, planning guides, and job aids. You'll use these resources to structure your presentations, to ensure clear communication, and to build client confidence.

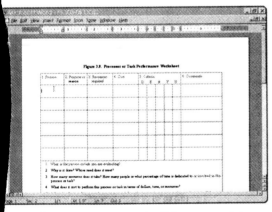

Among the many resources on the diskette are worksheets you'll use to manage your resources!

The Fieldbook enables you to:

- *Analyze* an organizational environment
- *Diagnose* performance problems
- *Identify* barriers to performance
- *Select* appropriate interventions
- *Measure* intervention success . . . and much more!

Employees don't need to learn more; they need to perform better. And as a per-formance consultant armed with Hale's *Fieldbook*, you will have the tools you need to effect measurable enhancements in performance.

Make the transition to performance consultant today!

> **"Everyone in the performance improvement industry should have a copy of Hale's book sitting on their desk for easy reference at all times."**
> —Gwen Nichols-White, training manager, Siemens Medical Systems

About the Author

Judith Hale is the president of Hale Associates, a consulting firm specializing in performance management, performance improvement systems, and strategic planning. She has contributed to or edited many published works, including *Designing Work Groups, Jobs, and Work Flow* (1995) and *Designing Cross-Functional Business Processes* (1995), both published by Jossey-Bass, as well as *The Guidebook for Performance Improvement* (Jossey-Bass/Pfeiffer, 1997). The recipient of several professional awards and honors, Hale is an active member of both ASTD and ISPI.

hardcover / 256 pages / includes Microsoft Word diskette
••••••••••••••••••••••••
The Performance Consultant's Fieldbook
Item #F508

Even Trainers Need Training!

Karen Lawson

Train-the-Trainer

Facilitator's Guide and The Trainer's
Handbook

Facilitator's Guide

The demand for training often exceeds the available
resources. That's when organizations turn to their
subject-matter experts. These employees often have
no training experience, but they have valuable infor-

**Remember—even trainers need
training! Build a solid foundation
for new trainers with this "total-
trainer" development workshop
and resource guide.**

mation to share with
their coworkers.
Usually, these sub-
ject-matter experts
are given little or no
formal instruction
on how to train. It's
sink or swim. They
struggle to convey their expertise, and their untu-
tored training can fall on unwilling ears.

The *Train-the-Trainer* workshop is the helping
hand that no new trainer can do without. The
Instructor's Guide gives you the tips, tools, checklists,
and guidelines you need to conduct an effective,
interactive train-the-trainer program.

You'll teach new trainers how to:

- *Conduct* a needs assessment
- *Identify* their training style
- *Design* their instructional plan
- *Use* active training techniques
- *Deliver* their training
- *Evaluate* their training . . . and much more!

Plus, this guide is packed with figures and
exhibits you'll use as overheads, flip charts, and
handouts. And the *Train-the-Trainer* workshop is

flexible: • the full program is 6 days, but if time and
money are limited, you can shorten the program
• the modules can be delivered on consecutive days,
or they may be distributed over several weeks. Pick
and choose! If your audience won't have any responsibility for conducting a needs assessment, the mod-
ular design of the *Train-the-Trainer* workshop allows
you to eliminate the needs assessment section from
the program. You'll have no problem making this
comprehensive program suit your training schedule!

The Trainer's Handbook

The Trainer's Handbook is a component of the workshop and a stand-alone resource. Both novice and
pro trainers—even if they haven't participated in the
workshop—will find this handbook indispensable!

New trainers will learn the basics, plus they'll get practical tips on:

- *Assessing* the attitudes of your participants
- *Keeping* your training learner-centered
- *Remaining* sensitive to the diversity of your
  audience
- *Incorporating* games into your training
- *Selecting* audio-visual aids
- *Closing* your sessions creatively . . . and more!

Facilitator's Guide / looseleaf / 300 pages • The Trainer's
Handbook / paperback / 240 pages

• •

Train-the-Trainer Facilitator's Guide
Item #F469

The Trainer's Handbook
Item #F470

"Practical, compassionate, and a good alternative to an MBA."

Peter Block, author, *Flawless Consulting*

Elaine Biech

The Business of Consulting

The Basics and Beyond

Lacking a basic primer, many consultants have had to learn their jobs by trial and error. Now you can put an end to the guesswork. This how-to book gives you the actual tools and techniques you need in order to pursue a successful and profitable career in the world of consulting.

This book is sure to become a consulting classic!

"Here are the nuts and bolts for a successful career in consulting. A few hours with Elaine's book will save you years of trial and error."
—Jerry C. Noack, vice president/group publisher, *TRAINING Magazine*

"If I were just starting into the consulting field today, this is the one book I would choose to advise me, caution me, support me in my business, and 'professionalize' me!"
—Marjorie Blanchard, chief financial officer, Blanchard International

"Every consultant should apply her principled practices to guarantee satisfied customers."
—John E. Gherty, president and chief executive officer, Land O'Lakes

"This book is filled with real-world, practical and proven tactics that can be used to grow and build a successful consulting practice. It is a must-have resource for people who are thinking of becoming a consultant—and for those who already are one!"
—Dana Gaines Robinson, author; president, Partners in Change

"Read her book. She shares all her secrets!"
—Gail Hammack, regional vice president, McDonald's

"The Business of Consulting will serve as my consulting practice workbook. The comprehensive coverage of the subject—along with the practical tips—make it the best tool I have."
—Pam Schmidt, vice president, American Society for Training and Development (ASTD)

There's more to consulting than just being a good consultant. You've got to manage your business.

When Elaine Biech asked Peter Block, the legendary author of *Flawless Consulting*, for a book or article that might answer some of her questions about running a consulting business, he could suggest no resource. There wasn't a source that illuminated the day-to-day life of a consultant. You learned by trial and error. Or you begged your peers for advice.

That was then; this is now. Here's the book that all consultants, new and old, have desperately needed.

Biech shows you how to:

- *Develop* a business plan
- *Market* your business
- *Charge* for your services
- *Build* a client relationship
- *Grow* your consulting business
- *Ensure* your continued professional growth
- *Make* money in the profession . . . and much more!

FREE diskette inc
sample invoic
corresponden
planning templ
and more!

The enclosed disk contains the worksheets and forms presented in *The Business of Consulting*. Personalize these tools as needed and print them out in order to project cash flow, track your time, tabulate your expenses, hire a subcontractor, plan your marketing campaigns, and much more!

Whether you're embarking on a new career as a consultant or whether you've been a consultant for years, you'll be able to employ this resource right away. And if you're deciding whether consulting is the right profession for you, *The Business of Consulting* will show you just what you can expect to encounter. For years, consultants have depended on Peter Block's *Flawless Consulting* for advice on being an effective consultant. Now there's a source for advice on running an effective consulting business—*The Business of Consulting* is indispensable.

About the Author

Elaine Biech, the author of more than a dozen articles and books, is president and managing principal of ebb associates inc. Biech has been in the consulting field for seventeen years and has developed training packages for health care institutions; the insurance, banking, and shipbuilding industries; manufacturing companies; and government and nonprofit organizations.

hardcover / 208 pages / includes a Microsoft Word diskette

• • • • • • • • • • • • • • • • • •
The Business of Consulting
Item #F510

all the material at once, or distribute it over several modules.

The *Handbook* reinforces key workshop concepts. Even novice and pro facilitators who haven't participated in the workshop will find this resource guide essential. The *Handbook* details key facilitation methods, offers step-by-step instructions for facilitating meetings, and much more. Numerous checklists and forms enable quick implementation.

Remember, the *Handbook* is an essential tool even for professionals who haven't participated in a *Facilitator Excellence* workshop. This standalone facilitation reference is a gold mine of tips and tools.

The *Profile* assesses facilitators' abilities and suggests areas for improvement. Incorporated into the *Facilitator Excellence* workshop, this quick assessment is also an effective follow-up tool that ensures ongoing facilitator development.

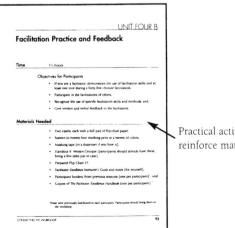

Useful handouts can be photocopied for easy distribution

Fran Rees

Facilitator Excellence

Instructor's Guide, Handbook, and Profile

Today's organizations are using teams to carry out tasks and solve problems. To get the job done, your managers and team leaders need to communicate and cooperate. Facilitation is the skill that saves the day! This workshop shows your employees how to become effective facilitators, and enables them to develop this skill in others. Great facilitators promote employee commitment and satisfaction, and augment team performance and problem solving. And flawless facilitation starts with *Facilitator Excellence*.

The *Instructor's Guide* includes everything you need to conduct a facilitation workshop: simulations, discussion resources, and more. The flexible workshop is organized around practical problems, so participants never lose sight of the job. You can deliver

Practical activities reinforce material

This package helps professionals to:
- *Lead* meetings effectively
- *Organize* team activities
- *Obtain* project support
- *Find* solutions to problems
- *Establish* harmony among coworkers
- *Deal* with customers and clients
- *Set* goals and make decisions
- *Earn* support for initiatives . . . and much more!

You'll need one copy of the *Instructor's Guide* for the trainer, skilled facilitator, or manager who will conduct the workshop. Each participant will need one copy of the *Handbook* and the *Profile*.

Instructor's Guide / looseleaf / 256 pages • Handbook / paperback / 240 pages • Profile / 16 pages

•••••••••••

Instructor's Guide
Item #F318

Handbook
Item #F319

Profile
Item #F320

Printed in the United Kingdom by
Lightning Source UK Ltd., Milton Keynes
139374UK00001B/22/A